CW00507044

PROFESSIONAL IMAGE:
Your Roadmap to SUCCESS

YOUR PERSONAL JOURNEY TO ENHANCING
YOUR STATUS AND CAREER BY LOOKING,
SOUNDING AND BEHAVING PROFESSIONALLY

ST Training Solutions
Success Skills Series

PANG LI KIN AICI CIP

PROFESSIONAL IMAGE:
Your Roadmap to SUCCESS

YOUR PERSONAL JOURNEY TO ENHANCING
YOUR STATUS AND CAREER BY LOOKING,
SOUNDING AND BEHAVING PROFESSIONALLY

Marshall Cavendish
Business

© 2010 Marshall Cavendish International (Asia) Private Limited
© text Pang Li Kin
© series title Shirley Taylor
Illustrations by Edwin Ng
Cover art by Opal Works Co. Limited

Published by Marshall Cavendish Business
An imprint of Marshall Cavendish International
1 New Industrial Road, Singapore 536196

Other Marshall Cavendish Offices:
Marshall Cavendish International. PO Box 65829 London EC1P 1NY, UK · Marshall Cavendish Corporation. 99 White Plains Road, Tarrytown NY 10591-9001, USA · Marshall Cavendish International (Thailand) Co Ltd. 253 Asoke, 12th Flr, Sukhumvit 21 Road, Klongtoey Nua, Wattana, Bangkok 10110, Thailand · Marshall Cavendish (Malaysia) Sdn Bhd, Times Subang, Lot 46, Subang Hi-Tech Industrial Park, Batu Tiga, 40000 Shah Alam, Selangor Darul Ehsan, Malaysia.

Marshall Cavendish is a trademark of Times Publishing Limited

Pang, Li Kin-
Professional image : your roadmap to success / Pang Li Kin. — Singapore : Marshall Cavendish Business, c2010.
p. cm. – (Success skills series)
Includes index.
ISBN-13 : 978-981-4276-28-3

1. Success in business. 2. Self-presentation. 3. Business etiquette. 4. Clothing and dress.
I. Title. II. Series: Success skills series (ST Training Solutions)

HF5386
650.1 — dc22   OCN498034848

Printed by Times Printers Pte Ltd

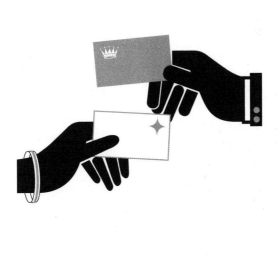

ACKNOWLEDGEMENTS

This book would not have been possible without Shirley Taylor, the Series Editor of the Success Skills Series of books. I am grateful to Shirley for giving me the honour to be one of the authors in her immensely successful series, without which I would still be dreaming about writing a book. Shirley was not only an excellent editor, she was also a source of encouragement and motivation, and made my writing so much more enjoyable and fulfilling.

In some ways, this book is a result of my journey through two major career paths: one in the marketing research industry, and the other as an Image Professional now. I am deeply indebted to my colleagues, bosses and clients who have taught me precious lessons about personal leadership and success, providing me with the foundation upon which I have built my Professional Image business.

On this note, I want to thank Lynne Marks AICI CIM from whom I learnt the fundamentals of running an Image business. She was my inspiration and helped me believe I could start a new career at the age of 50! I also thank all my clients who believed in me and supported me all these years.

Last but not least, thank you to my husband Lawrence and daughters Amanda, Liana and Amelia, for their love and patience with the workaholic in me!

Pang Li Kin AICI CIP
Founding Director, Potenxia Unlimited
www.potenxia.com

PREFACE

Congratulations on picking up this copy of *Professional Image: Your Roadmap to Success*. I'm very proud to include this in the ST Training Solutions Success Skills Series. This series includes several short, practical books on a range of topics that will help you develop your skills and enhance your success at work and in your personal life too.

The Success Skills series was originally created to meet the needs of participants of ST Training Solutions public workshops. After attending our workshops, many participants expressed a real desire to continue learning, to find out more about the topic, to take it to another level. They were hungry for knowledge. Just the effect I hoped for when I set up ST Training Solutions in 2007. With the Success Skills series of books, the experience and expertise of our trainers can be enjoyed by many more people.

As Series Editor, I've enjoyed working with the authors to make sure the books are easy-to-read, highly practical, and written in straightforward, simple language. Every book is packed with essential tools and strategies that will make you more effective and successful. We've included illustrations throughout that reinforce some key points, because I believe we learn more if we add some fun and humour. You'll also notice some key features that highlight important learning points:

Myth Buster

Here you will find a statement that is not true, with notes on the true facts of the matter.

Fast Fact

Useful snippets of information or special points to remember.

Aha! Moment

This is a 'light bulb' moment, when we note something you may be able to conclude from a discussion. Don't forget to note your own 'Aha! Moments' perhaps when you receive some extra insight that clarifies an important point.

Try This

Here you'll find a suggestion for how you can put a special point into practice, either at home or at work.

Danger Zone

You'll find some words of warning here, such as things to avoid or precautions to take.

Star Tips

At the end of each chapter you'll find a list of Star Tips — important notes to remind you about the key points.

By picking up this book you have already shown a desire to learn more. The solid advice and practical guidelines provided in this book will show you how you can really go from good to great!

Good luck!

Shirley Taylor
Series Editor
CEO, ST Training Solutions Pte Ltd

 ST Training Solutions

www.shirleytaylortraining.com
www.shirleytaylor.com

CONTENTS

INTRODUCTION

Most of us spend a good one-fifth of our lives preparing for the day we can be financially independent and carve a career to make us wealthy, famous or powerful. We remember our parents nagging us to study hard so that we can get a good job and support ourselves. Some of us would grudgingly do our homework, and some would find the lamest excuse not to do so, while yet others (lucky souls!) could amazingly score distinctions with their eyes closed.

Whether we end up a scholar, a dropout, or just an average student, our desire is the same — we want a successful career to be financially independent. While we may end up in different occupations because of our different academic inclinations, there is one driving force that determines our success. It is not taught in schools or the university, and you need not be a genius to obtain it. Neither do you need to be rich or good-looking for that matter.

I believe this driving force is your professional image. Your professional image is projected through the way you look, sound and behave at work. It determines how you will influence the way potential employers or customers perceive your best qualities, and their decision to hire you or buy from you. Whatever your qualifications and experience, your image will make a big difference in whether you get your foot in the door first, and are top of the list of preferred choice when the next promotion is due.

This book will show you how to let your image work for you. Whether you are just entering the workforce or looking for a new career direction, you will find it useful for developing a strong professional image for your future success.

I believe you are born beautiful, and I will show you how to bring out that beauty in your professional image. Your professional image is not just your appearance, but also the way you communicate. I will also demonstrate how your image is reflected in your personality, and how it impacts your behaviour at work.

I've included some stories and lessons that I feel will benefit you. I think you will enjoy them if you treat them as part of the overall journey. Take your time to chart your roadmap, practise the tips and guidelines, and use the tools and techniques. Take notes along the way, and mark the spots you may like to revisit. Stop to ponder and review your progress at the end of each chapter. Take a short-cut to the next chapters if the urge is there. However, if you feel the need to take a break from the book, you could be facing a roadblock, and if that happens, go to the last chapter where you will find some ideas to bring you back on track!

Have a safe and pleasant journey, and I wish you success in finding your pot of gold at the end of the book.

Pang Li Kin AICI CIP
www.potenxia.com

ASSESS YOURSELF

What's your current understanding of professional image?

1.   What represents a professional image?

a)   The way you look represents your work and your organisation well.

b)   The way you speak conveys a clear message of your values.

c)   The way you behave reflects well on your position.

d)   All of the above.

2.   Before you embark on an image makeover, you must know:

a)   How much it costs, and whether you can afford to change your whole wardrobe.

b)   Who are the best image consultants in your location.

c)   What are your vision and goals to create the image you want.

d)   All of the above.

3.   You can look professional by:

a)   Wearing what's appropriate in your profession, organisation and culture.

b)   Wearing a power suit.

c)   Wearing formal colours like black and white.

d)   Answers (b) and (c).

4.   When is it not appropriate to wear red at work?

a)   To an interview or job appraisal with your boss.

b)   When you are making a presentation.

c)   At your company's anniversary celebration.

d)   When you need to grab attention and be in control.

5. Which of the following is an acceptable professional behaviour?

a) Giving confidential pricing information to your suppliers.

b) Just say, "It's the company's policy" when you cannot give a customer what he wants.

c) Taking responsibility for a mistake committed by your team member.

d) Buying pirated software to save your company's money.

6. If your voice sounds monotonous and boring, what can you do?

a) Tell more jokes to engage the audience.

b) Have more discussions so that you don't have to speak so much.

c) Your content is more important, so don't do anything to your voice.

d) Add some drama to your voice by changing your tone, speed or volume.

7. How do you project a professional image in your resumé?

a) Provide a professional photograph.

b) Give all the details of your education and experience — the more details, the better.

c) Don't state your expected salary.

d) Customise the content and presentation to the needs of your potential employer.

8. An effective way to let your boss notice how outstanding you are is to:

a) Dress to impress — it's the only way.

b) Establish relationship with colleagues and stakeholders within the organisation.

c)   Tell people how good you are so the boss gets to hear about it.

d)   All of the above.

9.   What do you do if your colleagues criticise you for dressing better than they do?

a)   Feel flattered, as they must be poorly dressed.

b)   Dress like them so you won't feel out of place.

c)   Don't mix with them, as they are not worthy of your company.

d)   Gain their support by getting feedback on how your dressing might work for you.

10.   To create a working wardrobe without spending a fortune, you need to:

a)   Have one basic black jacket.

b)   Buy from factory outlets and shop during sales only.

c)   Buy an item only if it works with three other items in your wardrobe.

d)   Buy matching outfits so you don't need to mix and match.

Check out these answers to see how you fared.

1.   The correct answer is (d). Having a professional image is not about appearance only. Your look, sound and behaviour must convey the same message about who you are and what you represent. Find out more about how this works in Chapters 1 and 3.

2.   Did you answer (d)? Sorry! You must know what your image for the future will look like before an image consultant can help you scope the makeover required, so answer (c) is the correct answer. To chart your personal vision and goals for your professional image, go to Chapter 2.

3. What looks professional for someone may not look professional for you, so (a) is the correct answer here. You can dress professionally by using the appropriate styles and colour for your own profession and organisation. Learn more in Chapters 4 and 5.

4. Red is an exciting, energetic and stimulating colour, so all answers except (a) are incorrect. Check out the significance and messages of different colours in Chapter 5.

5. You're right if you answered (c). While the other answers reflect common behaviours at the workplace, it doesn't mean they are acceptable. Assess your behaviour in Chapter 3, and identify what represents professional behaviour in Chapter 7.

6. No matter how great your content is, you need a powerful voice to grab attention. Your voice can be trained to create the impact you want, so (d) is the correct answer. To enhance your vocal quality, try out some exercises in Chapter 6.

7. The correct answer is (d). Recruiters spend less than 10 seconds reviewing a resumé, so yours will stand out if you address the needs of your potential employer. Take a lesson to beef up your resumé in Chapter 8.

8. Physical appearance and what people say about you are insufficient to show how outstanding you are. (b) is the answer I am looking for. Find out how you can be noticed and remembered in Chapter 9.

9. The best way to address criticism is to use it as feedback, so the answer is (d). To address this and other roadblocks, turn to Chapter 10.

10. To make your wardrobe work for you, every item should be maximised. You are right if you chose answer (c). Find out how to do this by using the *capsule* concept in Chapter 4.

IMAGE BUILDS SUCCESS

"Even before we speak, we are condemned or approved."

Dale Carnegie

Imagine you are walking into an interview room, and before you have a chance to answer the first question, the employer has already made up his mind about hiring you!

Imagine you are meeting a potential client for the first time, and before you open your PowerPoint presentation, she has already decided whether she's going to buy from you or not!

It may sound unfair and harsh, but it can happen to you. We may not want to admit it, but we do this to others, and others do it to us. I have a confession to make. When I was an Executive Director at the then-ACNielsen Company in the 1990s, on more than one occasion I hired new staff on the spot before I finished interviewing all the candidates. One of them was my super-efficient secretary, Joyce, who was completely shocked when I told her at the end of the interview that she had got the job! There were also a couple of executives who I decided to hire immediately and they turned out to be among the best and most successful executives our team ever had.

Was I unfair? I believe these employees are grateful that I made such swift judgement about them. They may not know this, but it was based on the first impression they created — and it was not just about their appearances, it was the *image* they projected. We will establish in this chapter what a professional image means and how this will build success for your career.

The impact of your image on success

While success is dependent on many different factors, there is enough evidence in the real world around us to suggest that it pays to take care of how we project ourselves. Researchers have found that employers do take appearance into account when hiring or promoting employees. According to James Andreoni and Ragan Petrie in the *Journal of Economic Psychology* published in 2007, "Attractive people make more money than middle attractive people, who in turn make more money than unattractive people".

Fast Fact

Research shows that even accounting for intelligence, income is enhanced by appearance. All things being equal, statistics have shown that attractive people earn 12 per cent more than unattractive people.

Now, I'm not saying that talent and skills are not important. Of course they are. In today's job market, qualifications, experience and competencies are minimum expectations. Your employer, colleagues, customers and potential customers expect you to perform based on your job position and credentials. The bad news is this: you are not the only one in the whole wide world with the same job and qualifications. Employers and clients have a choice — in economic boom or in recession — they can choose to hire you, fire you, buy from you, or buy from someone else.

The truth is, we all make judgements on people we have not met before based on our first impressions of them. For example, let's suppose a middle-aged man walks into your office wearing a t-shirt with big gaudy prints worn loosely over dirty, faded denim jeans. Who would you think he is? Would your first thought be, "He must be a delivery man or technician" or "He's a senior executive from a client company"? Even before he speaks, you have probably already decided that he's a delivery man, right? No one would blame you for that. We are all guilty of judging people by their appearance, even though we know it's not a fair thing to do!

In the same way, you are being judged every day based on your appearance. What are people thinking when they see you dressed the way you do? We are not just talking about people in the office, as you are seen by hundreds of people when you are on your way to work, in the bus, train, in the elevator, at lunchtime and after work. Are you noticed, or, are you just another digit in the working population? What if one of them was a potential employer or client who could help you make a million dollars?

If we make a bad first impression, we have to work very hard to change it, but if we make a consistently good impression, it is easier for others to accept us. This can only help to open doors to opportunities that will eventually lead to greater success.

Aha! Moment

I don't have a second chance with first impressions. Once people form a certain impression of me that I do not intend to project, it results in missed opportunities.

What is image?

Despite the research, I'd like to make a distinction here between good looks and image. While researchers have attempted to use an objective measure on what is deemed 'attractive' and 'good looks', the reality is that beauty is subjective. We have all heard the saying that "beauty is in the eye of the beholder", and we all have personal experiences to support this. As an Image Professional, I truly believe we are all born beautiful. The problem with some people, however, is that they make themselves unattractive by wearing clothes that sabotage themselves.

So here's the good news: we can all look attractive by bringing out the beauty inside us. Image is not about having good looks, it is about looking good! This is within everyone's reach — the ability to look outstanding inside out!

Myth Buster

Only pageant queens and kings get the best jobs and pay! All my hard work and experience do not count.

We all know that's not true. Having a good image is not about having good looks; it is about reflecting your best qualities through your appearance, communication and behaviour. A consistently positive image keeps you top-of-mind when a new job, promotion or opportunity arises.

Image, then, is not just about your physical appearance alone. It has a lot more to do with who you are and what you represent, and how you project this in the way you dress, talk and behave. Image is about the messages you convey to others when they meet you and interact with you. They can be visual, verbal or non-verbal. We will discuss this in more detail in Chapters 6 and 7.

If you feel sloppy and carefree about the way you dress, you send out a silent and powerful message about the way you may be managing your life and work. There is also a halo effect: when you dress sloppily, you will also speak sloppily, and your posture will follow suit. On the other hand, if you feel confident about your clothes, hairstyle and personal presentation, you will send out a positive and confident message.

Fast Fact

In a survey of employers conducted in the United States, 95 per cent of employers said that a job seeker's personal appearance affected their opinion of the applicant's suitability for the post.

91 per cent of employers said they believed dress and grooming reflected the applicant's attitude towards the company.

61 per cent of employers said employees' dress and grooming had an effect on subsequent promotions.

So now we can see that image is much more than the physical aspects of our dressing and body language. What usually happens is when people see your physical 'package' they read the messages it conveys and they make a judgement about your attitude, experience and competence. They then respond to you by acting on that judgement, i.e. to hire you or buy from you. If their experience with you confirms this initial judgement, then their action is justified.

Aha! Moment

So I don't need to wear an Armani suit when I attend a job interview! What a relief! To land my dream job, I need to dress appropriately to reflect the messages I wish to convey about my suitability for the job.

Your image is stored in a box

Whenever you meet someone, the messages you convey get captured like a picture and stored in a box in people's heads. It may be a pretty box or a dull brown box. The picture may be memorable or forgettable. It may evoke positive or negative feelings. Just like the folders you create on your computer for your various documents, these boxes get filed away in two main rooms — the positive room and the negative room.

1. **The positive room.** When you create a positive impression on someone, you will be stored in their positive room. This partly explains why *attractive* people have an edge over *unattractive* people — because when people look pleasant, it evokes a positive feeling. This is also why first impressions are often based on appearances, as they are formed within the first few seconds of meeting someone.

2. **The negative room.** When you send messages that are not consistent with your appearance or behaviour, people may be confused and hence they are more likely to put you in the negative room. They may wonder if you can really do what you claim you can do. People who do not take much care with their appearance will have to work doubly hard to prove themselves. When they do eventually prove themselves, they will move from the negative to the positive room.

So, what is harder, to shift from the positive to the negative or from negative to positive?

You are right if you said the latter. If people file you in the negative room based on one small bad experience, it will be much harder to get back into the positive room. This reinforces my point that your image must reflect who you are inside so what people see is what they get. If you are professional in the way you conduct yourself and do business, and if you look professional too, you will stay in the positive room all the time.

On the contrary, if your speech and behaviour is not consistent with your professional image, you will be transferred to the negative room and will stay there for a long time unless you change your speech and behaviour.

 Try This

If you were a 'box' stored in someone's head, what kind of a 'box' are you? Ask yourself these questions:

1. What does it look like? What colour is it? How is it wrapped?

2. What is inside the box? Do you see quality or quantity?

3. What is the feeling you get when you think of what's inside the box?

For more insights, you may wish to ask a friend to do the same for you, and exchange your thoughts on how you wish your box to look and feel.

What is professional image?

We have now established the importance of image and how it can affect your success. You should now be able to choose the kind of image you wish to project to achieve the success you want. I will take you step-by-step through charting your roadmap to success in Chapter 2. Here, let's first look at what is meant by having a professional image.

No matter our position or organisation, we must all be professional. When I was travelling in Japan recently, I was truly impressed to see two very well-groomed young ladies working as 'garbage collectors' in train stations. They wore clean, white uniforms with blue floral-print aprons and clean, crisp hats over very neat, well-groomed hair. They wore simple makeup and bright smiles. These ladies took garbage directly from passengers to put into the bin without us having to look for a bin (incidentally, there are hardly any waste bins outdoors in Japan). The ladies said "*arigato*" (which means "thank you") for dropping our garbage with them.

That is what I mean by creating a professional image. Whatever job you are doing, when you create a professional image, you make it easy and pleasant for people to work with you, and to want to do business with you in the future.

The three key elements of a professional image are:

Looking professional

Sounding professional

Behaving like a professional

Let's take a look at each of these three elements and see what it means to look, sound and behave professionally.

Looking professional

Looking professional does not mean you have to wear a power suit. All it means is that the way you dress should represent your work and your organisation well. If you work in the environment industry, you need to look clean, well-groomed and smell nice. If you are pitching for a million-dollar account, you need to look trustworthy, smart and competent.

Sounding professional

Similarly, whatever language you speak, you need to represent your work and your organisation well. If you are a sales person, you need to sound confident, knowledgeable and polite. If you work in the education industry, you must be articulate and polished in your speech.

Behaving professionally

This has to do with the way you conduct yourself, whether at work or outside of it. It means behaving in a manner that reflects well on your character and on your organisation. If you work for a public relations firm, you should be polished in your business etiquette and social skills. If you are a secretary or administrative professional, you are expected to be punctual, detail-oriented and well-organised (even in your personal life).

 Danger Zone

Once you've made a good first impression, it does not mean you need not care about your image anymore. If your future is important to you, maintaining a positive image all the time will open up new opportunities and possibilities. If you dress well for an interview, and then look dreadful after you get the job, you reduce your chances of advancing in your career.

Making a lasting impression

While much has been written about first impressions, we need to be mindful that these alone will not make you an overnight success. Indeed, I'm sure you have sometimes made a wrong judgement about someone based on first impressions, and later changed your mind based on further experience with them. This is where I must make my second confession: I have made mistakes in hiring people based on a great first impression, only to find out later that they were not suitable for the job at all!

So what happened? On reflection, while the applicants gave me a very good impression at the interview, they did not live up to the image they projected. It was as simple as that. It could happen to anyone. In other words, they did not make a lasting impression — they looked the part, but they did not act the part. The moment I realised this, I moved them from the positive to the negative room.

FIRST DAY AT WORK

ONE WEEK LATER

POSITIVE

NEGATIVE

Stay in the positive room with a consistent message

If you want to stay in the positive room, your image must be consistent. Consistency means having a standard below which you will not descend. On a day-to-day basis, your image needs to match who you are, i.e. internal consistency, as well as your environment, i.e. external consistency.

Internal consistency

When your image matches who you really are, and reflects you at your best every day, whether you are at work or play, this is internal consistency. To make this easy to remember, I have summed it up in the integrated triangles in the following diagram, which I call the VABC consistency model.

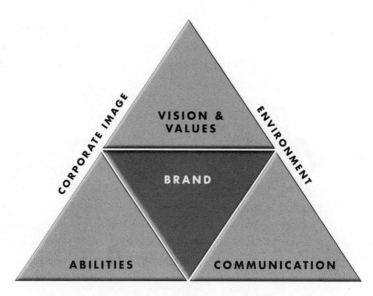

THE VABC CONSISTENCY MODEL

V: Vision and Values. Your vision has to do with where you want to go and what's important to you. For example, if you want to achieve excellence in your career, and quality is important to you, you would also reflect quality in your choice of clothes.

A: Abilities. This has to do with your skills and capabilities, and if you have what it takes to get where you want to go. If not, the image you try to project is not consistent and will not last. This brings us back to the point that underlying your image is an assumption that you are really what you project yourself to be. Otherwise, you are just faking it.

B: Brand. Your image must reflect what you stand for as well as your best qualities, i.e. your personal brand. If you are approachable and spontaneous, you will reflect this by more relaxed dressing and yet still look professional.

C: Communication. Your speech must be consistent with the image you project. This has to do with not just your language but also the way you speak, and the content. If what you say is hollow and superficial, it will not have a lasting impression on people.

External consistency

While internal consistency is very much within your control, external consistency calls for you to adapt to your corporate image and the environment in which you work. Take a moment to consider the culture and environment where you work: If it's conservative, traditional and formal, you will need to look, sound and behave more formally at business meetings and functions. If your environment is more forward-looking, modern and progressive, then you need to project a more up-to-date and upbeat image.

If your image is not consistent with your organisation's image and environment, a number of things could happen:

- Your boss and colleagues may think you don't fit in.

- You won't feel comfortable or confident in their presence.

- Your customers/vendors may not find you credible and will not want to do business with you.

When any of these things happen, your performance will be affected and you may quit your job thinking that you are not appreciated. However, the bottom line may be that the problems have nothing to do with your capabilities, and more to do with your image.

Armed with this realisation, you will be pleased to know that all of this can be changed! As you progress through the pages of this book, you will learn how to create an image that projects your individuality as well as that of your organisation — in a lasting way! I will help you create a professional image that will reflect your best qualities and those of your organisation. You will find that when your image is consistent with your internal values and qualities, as well as your external environment, you will become credible and believable. Your look, speech and behaviour will send a consistent message about who you are, and people will respond to you accordingly. As a result, you are sure to achieve much greater success. And that's a promise!

Star Tips for creating a successful image

1. Create a good first impression to get a head-start in your career.

2. Give special attention to your appearance when meeting someone for the first time.

3. Decide what message you wish to convey to others before you decide on your appearance.

4. Reflect your best qualities and those of your organisation so that you look professional.

5. Dress in a way that represents your work and your organisation well.

6. Speak in a manner that reflects the professionalism of your work and your organisation.

7. Behave in a way that creates an image of a professional representative of your company.

8. Create an image that is consistent with your personal vision, abilities, brand and communication.

9. Align your image with your company's image and environment.

10. Leave a lasting impression by being consistent in the way you look, sound and behave.

YOUR IMAGE ROADMAP: PRESENT, PAST AND FUTURE

"If you don't know where you are going, you will probably end up somewhere else."

Dr Laurence J Peter

When clients come to me for an image makeover, two questions I always ask them are what their goals are and what they want to get out of an image consultation. If the answer is, "I just want to change my image" or "I want to look gorgeous", then I know we are dealing with just physical appearances. To go beyond the physical aspects of image, you need to know what your goals are, and then determine what image you need to *change* into. If not, you may end up looking like someone else.

In this chapter, I will take you step-by-step through how you can chart a roadmap to help you achieve your goals for your professional image. For this to work, it will require some soul-searching and an honest review of your personal and professional life. You may find it uncomfortable at times as we go into your past, but if you are determined to start this new journey with me, I urge you to walk with me in good faith. Take as much time as you need, and complete each step in this chapter before you move on to the rest of the book.

Your personal image roadmap

Think of your personal image roadmap as a directory map in a shopping mall: when you refer to it, you first look for the red dot that says "you are here". The next thing you look for is where you came from, and also your destination (perhaps a shop or restaurant). Armed with these three points, you now can chart the direction and the route to your destination, or plan your trip to visit other shops along the way.

Charting your personal image roadmap is similar, except that you start with a blank sheet of paper and you have to draw the map yourself. The next steps require you to reflect on your present, past and future directions.

Try This

Take a large piece of drawing paper (drawing block or flipchart paper), crayons or marker pens, and any other creative tools (stickers, coloured paper, glitter glue, etc). Be as creative as you like, and draw a roadmap to represent your career, from the start to the future. It can be a straight narrow road or a long winding road.

Now mark a spot where you think you are right now: are you at a crossroads, on the highway, or in the parking lot?

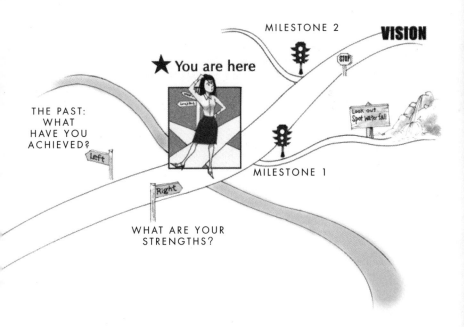

The present: where are you now?

When you are lost and checking out a map or street directory, you have to know where you are on the map before you can figure the way to your destination. If you have no clue where you are, the best maps in the world cannot help you.

When it comes to charting your personal image roadmap, this is the most essential step. If you have decided on the greatest destination (i.e. your dream career), this is no use if you do not know where you are right now. Fortunately, this is also the easiest step. However, this is the step that is usually missed when people are talking about their dream career. This is what I call the 'reality check', and most of the time the dream career remains a dream because we did not check on where we are now.

 Aha! Moment

Knowing where I am right now is critical to finding the direction to where I want to go. I cannot decide how far my career can go unless I know where I am right now in my career path.

Now return to the blank roadmap you just drew, and where you have marked the spot, list down all the facts about where you are in relation to your career. Avoid descriptions (e.g. "I'm the best secretary in the office") or connotations of success or failure (e.g. "I achieved my sales target" or "I'm not earning enough"). Instead, be factual and state what is the current situation for each of the following:

- **Your job status** (e.g. employed as an administrative manager for five years). This may seem like a pointless fact but it is a *huge* reality check for some people! In this case, you may realise that five years in the same role is a long time and puts you in good stead for a promotion or move up the career ladder. Or, if your job status is unemployed for six months, you need to act quickly to change that.

- **Your monthly income.**   Include income derived from external sources (e.g. allowance from your parents or spouse). This is all the money you have for you to spend or save. Again, it is a reality check of how much income you have and where it is coming from. As we move on to the next checkpoint, you will soon realise if this income is adequate for your current and future lifestyle.

- **Your monthly expenses.**   Be honest and include everything you are supposed to pay for. For credit card bills, take an average of the past 12 months (include the amount even if you are rolling over your bills).

- **Your dependants.**   List down all the people who depend on you for a living. Include only current dependants or in the near future (e.g. if you are expecting a new addition to the family). These people may need to be included in your journey as you chart your roadmap.

- **What's important to you?**   Write down everything that matters to you, which can include your work and personal life. Be honest here, so if wealth is important, write it down. Everything that is important to you will determine what your future will look like.

The past: what have you achieved?

Just like in the mall directory you must figure out where you came from before you can decide which direction to take. So, the next step is to mark some milestones prior to the spot where you are on your roadmap, and list down all your past achievements. Again, be factual and list down the major milestones that could have a significant impact on your future directions. These can include:

- **Educational achievements.** Include academic, professional or technical qualifications. Some careers require academic qualifications and some do not, so it is good to know if you have what it takes to achieve your dream career. If not, this will help you to identify any further education or training you need.

- **Work experience.** Include part-time jobs or even volunteer work if they are significant for you. Some job positions require relevant work experience (e.g. managerial positions), so you know what work experience you need to build up before you can reach your goal of, say, a manager.

- **Skills.** Include operational, technical or special skills that are usually acquired through training or practice. These can help determine your unique contribution to an organisation or business.

- **Awards.** Include any official recognition of your achievement or contribution as they indicate you have gained public acknowledgement in your field.

 Fast Fact

Skills are not the same as interests: you may be interested in tennis and watch every tournament, but not actually play tennis at all. Skills can be talents and abilities you have that may not have been maximised at work and may have potential for your future career. They can include artistic, language, IT, sports, technical or organisational skills.

What are your strengths?

Now that you have assessed your past and present, we are almost ready to look at what your future holds. Before we take this next step, I'd like you to take a breather to review the roadmap you have completed so far. Go down your two lists (from pages 20–22) and think of attributes that describe your strengths. Don't be modest, but at the same time, be honest!

Make as long a list as you can, and then try to group similar attributes together until you narrow them down to three key attributes. These three words will represent your brand values, and they will describe what your 'box' is really like inside.

Try This

This exercise will help you to identify your personal brand values.

Review your present and past achievements, and think of positive words that describe how well you have done. For example, if you have introduced new procedures in the office, you may say you are *innovative*. Here are some words to help you:

Approachable	Easy-going	Knowledgeable
Artistic	Energetic	Mature
Articulate	Enthusiastic	Motivated
Confident	Ethical	Progressive
Considerate	Friendly	Persuasive
Creative	Fun	Responsible
Dedicated	Generous	Reliable
Driven	Helpful	Supportive
Dynamic	Innovative	Thoughtful

Select three words that best describe your strengths. These are your brand values. Write them here.

1._____

2._____

3._____

Write these words on your mirror or screen saver to remind yourself every day of your personal brand values. This will inspire you to greater heights.

The future: where are you going?

By now, you may be wondering if we have digressed from the issue of how to create a professional image. This brings us back to the point about knowing what your goals are before we can work on your image. The main reason why people feel the need for a new image is because they have been projecting an image of the past or present. It may not necessarily be a bad image, but what they need is to project an image of their future.

Aha! Moment

You may have been projecting an image of the past if you have been successful in your previous career, i.e. your appearance and behaviour worked for you then. To raise your game and move to a new level, you may need to review your past image and see if this is holding you back from achieving more.

To project an image of your future, you need to set a vision and some goals: in other words, you need to know where your destination point is on your roadmap. So let's return to your roadmap and put the three key attributes at your destination point. Now, review what you have written down on your roadmap so far and create a vision statement on your destination point. This vision statement represents your future, so take your time to craft this. If it helps, take a walk or do some meditation so you can ponder over this before you write it down.

Crafting your personal vision

A vision statement provides a clear and vivid picture of an ideal situation in your future. There is no right or wrong vision so long as you believe it is achievable. In a school essay I wrote in the late 1960s, on the topic "What the future looks like", I described a vision of future transportation where people would just step on to a moving platform along the roads. They would get on and off without having to be in a vehicle. It was vivid and clear. It had an ideal situation. It was future-oriented and I believed it was achievable, although I didn't know how. When I saw the first travelator 15 years later at the Singapore Changi Airport, it reminded me of the vision I had. I am still hoping that one day we will see travelators on sidewalks!

Try This

If you find it hard to create a vision, close your eyes and try to recall a pleasant childhood memory. What do you see? Who are the people involved? What is the scenery like? What colours can you see? What sounds do you hear?

If you can see a vivid picture of the past, then a vision is simply a similar picture of the future. Once you can see a picture of you and what you are doing in the future, you can begin to write the vision statement down.

To polish your vision statement so it sounds inspiring, you can use any of the following methods:

- **Metaphor.** You can use an animal, object or thing to represent your vision. For example, a giraffe can represent a vision of 'towering above all others', and this may inspire you to write a vision statement that says 'To be the Tower of IT Solutions'. For me, my metaphor is an exponential graph (this represents rapid growth after a seemingly slow growth initially) and it represents my vision to 'transform the ordinary into extraordinary results' for my clients.

- **Simile.** This is used to compare two different objects, e.g. my mother-in-law is as gentle as a lamb (not that she is a lamb, but that she has the qualities of a lamb). It is useful to compare your qualities/yourself to another object or thing to highlight your unique strengths. For example, if your vision is to provide the fastest courier service in the world, your vision statement can be 'to be as fast as lightning'.

- **Analogy.** This compares similar characteristics of two dissimilar things, e.g. learning presentation skills is like riding a bicycle. In both cases, to do it well, you have to just keep practicing. If your vision is to help people deliver great presentations, the cyclist analogy may inspire you to want "to create champions in the speaking circuit".

Setting your goals and future milestones

Once you have noted your vision down on your roadmap, you can now see a line connecting the three points: your past, present and future. Now, we can move on to complete this roadmap by setting goals and milestones you need to reach your destination. If not, you may wish to revisit any of the three points to align them before you chart the rest of your roadmap.

While your vision is idealistic and future-oriented, your goals need to be specific and time-sensitive. If you believe your vision is achievable, then your goals must lead to this. Going back to the example of the mall directory, you may realise the journey to your destination is too long and you need stops along the way. So with your personal image roadmap, you can now set some goals as to where you can stop and for how long before you reach your destination, and still have time to get what you need.

On your paper, mark the milestones with time frames to indicate what goals need to be achieved to reach your vision. Consider your past achievements and your current status to determine what gaps exist between your present (where you are now) and your future (where you want to be). For example, if you are an administrative manager and have established yourself to be competent, innovative and efficient, and your vision is "to provide innovative solutions to human resource management", you may set the following goals:

1. Complete a diploma course in human resource management in two years' time.

2. Request posting to human resource department by _____ (year).

3. Set up in-house forums to gather employee feedback and develop solutions.

Danger Zone

Setting your vision and goals is more than just an exercise. If you are serious about projecting a professional image, you must be clear about your vision and goals. We can work with you to create an image that works for you only when you know where you wish the image to take you. Don't go for an image makeover before clarifying your goals with an image professional, otherwise you may end up with an image that does not align with your future career goals.

The vehicle to take you there

You now have a roadmap in place. What you need is a vehicle to take you there. I see your image as the vehicle: it is the means to an end. Having a professional image is never the end in itself. With your vision and goals in place, you now need to project an image that conveys the message, "I can do it!" So let's review this vehicle of yours: is it a vehicle of the past, present or future?

- ## What does it look like?

  Is it a hand-me-down or state-of-the-art vehicle to represent your future vision? Does your appearance remind you of your past (and how long ago was it)? If so, you may want to consider a look that represents your future career and vision. If you aspire to be a manager, then you may want to consider starting to dress like one. If you continue to look like a junior officer, people will continue to treat you like one and you may never be considered for a promotion.

- ## What does it sound like?

  When you rev your engine, does it sound like it needs some tuning or does it sound like it's made for the 21st century? Do your communication skills need polishing to get you where you need to go? If so, some sort of communication training should be one of the goals in your roadmap.

- **How does it behave?**

  Does the vehicle perform according to expectations of your past or future? Are you on manual gear or automatic drive? Does your behaviour convey outdated standards or are you constantly updating yourself? If you are out-of-touch with business etiquette for the future, you may need to include this as another goal for training.

- **Who are the passengers?**

  You may not be travelling alone as there may be important people in your life (or in your future) you must take along. Review the list of important things on your roadmap, and consider people who matter to you and affect your journey to your destination. If your dream career requires you to travel extensively, your goals may need to include planning for their lifestyle, or saving enough to include them in your travels.

 Myth Buster

A vision is too idealistic and cannot be achieved.

True only if you believe it to be. A vision is never *too* idealistic as it is something you *wish* to have or be, so it *is* achievable. Setting a vision gives you a destination, even if you are not sure how you can get there. Without knowing where you wish to go, you could remain stagnant (i.e. stay in the same job for decades) or you could move from job to job instead of landing a better job.

Let's start the engine!

The only way for your vehicle to get you to your destination is for you to start the engine and get going. If your vehicle needs servicing and there is a long journey ahead, you cannot ignore it. Similarly, if your image looks, sounds and behaves like the past, it's time to consider an overhaul. This is what an image makeover is really about.

Now, with a clear idea of where you are going, we can move on to the next step, which will show you how you can ride smoothly with a new professional image.

Star Tips for creating your personal roadmap

1. Be aware of the image you wish to project before you embark on an image makeover, otherwise you may end up looking like someone else.

2. Chart your roadmap to a professional image by identifying where you are, where you came from and what your destination is.

3. Assess your current situation and perform a reality check. This helps you realise how far you can go with your future career.

4. List down what's important to you in your pursuit of a dream career. These have an impact on how far you wish to go on this journey.

5. Review your past achievements. This will help you identify areas you can develop to take you to a higher level.

6. Map out your strengths based on your past achievements. Narrow them down to three attributes that describe you at your best.

7. Create a clear vision of your career in the future. It must have an ideal standard and yet be achievable. This stretches the possibilities for you and inspires you to keep raising the bar.

8. Set goals and milestones necessary to reach your vision. They must be specific and have a time frame.

9. Assess what your current image is like. Does it reflect the past, present or future? Your image needs to look, sound and behave like your future.

10. Make a commitment to boost your professional image to help you achieve your vision.

ASSESS YOUR PROFESSIONAL IMAGE: VSP INDEX

"You can't manage what you don't measure."

Author Unknown

3

Now that you have your roadmap charted out and are ready to take a bold step to make a change in your professional image, the next question is: what needs changing and by how much? It is easy to say, "I need an image makeover", but what exactly needs to be made over, and to what extent is change required?

Before you leap to the next chapters to find out how to create your best professional image, this chapter will help you to carefully assess your current image. Like corporations who need to measure their performances before they can manage their businesses, you too need to evaluate your current image in order to reach your goals. Without going through this stage, you may end up with an instant makeover that you get at a photo salon: they make you look fantastic for one moment in time and only for the camera. Then a few hours later you are back to being the other you again. What you really need is a new image that will take you to your *real* future and not just look good for a few moments in print.

The VSP index: Your visual, sound and personality impact

The VSP index is a simple composite measure of the three key components of your professional image:

Visual   How you look professionally

Sound   How you communicate professionally
                   (verbally and in writing)

Personality   How you behave professionally

Before you complete the VSP index, it will help if you review the three brand values you came up with in Chapter 2 (page 23) and use them as a yardstick to assess yourself. This requires you to be honest with yourself, and you do not need to show this to anyone if you don't wish to.

Myth Buster

A self-evaluation is biased since I will tend to think highly of myself and do not know whether others perceive the same about me.

You are right if you are rating yourself on a scale of excellent to poor and if you have a very high self-esteem. That's why this tool is designed to use your brand values and not your own standard as a yardstick. This helps you to be more objective and gives you an opportunity to take an honest look inside yourself. You are also right that your self-evaluation may differ from others' perception of you. When you ask others to rate you using this same tool, you will be able to address some blind spots about how your image is projected to others. We will discuss this in more detail later in this chapter.

The VSP index in practice

Here's an example of the VSP index to get you started: Supposing your three brand values are *progressive*, *approachable* and *creative*, how would you rate yourself on your visual appearance in terms of matching the brand values of being progressive, approachable and creative? If you regularly update your wardrobe and keep up with the trends, you can consider yourself to match your value of being *progressive*. If you demonstrate individuality in your style, you are also consistent with your value of being *creative*. If you tend to pick relaxed styles in contrast to formal dressing, you are projecting the image of being *approachable*. Overall, then, you can rate your visual appearance as being *exceptional* (rating of 10) in matching your brand values.

Don't worry about being precise on the rating; use your personal judgement based on what you perceive your brand values should be like. When in doubt, give a lower rating.

The VSP index and you

Rate yourself on the following attributes using a scale of 1 to 10, where '1' means it is inconsistent with your brand values and '10' means it is exceptional in matching your brand values.

THE VSP INDEX

Visual (How you look)										
1. Office attire (what you wear daily to work)	1	2	3	4	5	6	7	8	9	10
2. Formal attire (for official events or evening wear)	1	2	3	4	5	6	7	8	9	10
3. Business casual attire (for Friday casual or informal business events)	1	2	3	4	5	6	7	8	9	10
4. Grooming (hair, skin, body, etc)	1	2	3	4	5	6	7	8	9	10
5. Accessories (shoes, bags, ties and belts for men)	1	2	3	4	5	6	7	8	9	10
Sound (How you communicate)										
6. Verbal communication (phone and face-to-face conversations)	1	2	3	4	5	6	7	8	9	10
7. Written communication (email and business writing)	1	2	3	4	5	6	7	8	9	10
8. Listening skills (how attentive you are)	1	2	3	4	5	6	7	8	9	10
9. Presentations skills (how you convey an idea or thought to a group)	1	2	3	4	5	6	7	8	9	10
10. Non-verbal (body language like gestures, facial expressions, and tone of voice)	1	2	3	4	5	6	7	8	9	10
Personality (How you behave)										
11. Work habits (timeliness and work performance, etc)	1	2	3	4	5	6	7	8	9	10
12. Staff relationships (peers, subordinates and seniors)	1	2	3	4	5	6	7	8	9	10
13. External relationships (clients, suppliers, etc)	1	2	3	4	5	6	7	8	9	10
14. Business etiquette (manners at work, dining or networking)	1	2	3	4	5	6	7	8	9	10
15. Problem-handling (how you deal with difficult situations or people)	1	2	3	4	5	6	7	8	9	10

Fast Fact

Perception is real. How you perceive yourself affects the way you project yourself to others. How others perceive you affects the way they treat you.

How you scored on the VSP index

1. Add up your scores for each section and record under Raw Score in the boxes below.

2. Divide the raw score by 50 and then multiply by 100. This gives you the index for each section.

3. Add the three indices and divide by 3. This gives your overall VSP index.

	Raw Scores	Item Index (Divide by 50/Multiply by 100)
Visual:		
Sound:		
Personality:		
Total:		
Overall VSP Index (Divide Total by 3):		

How to interpret the scores

The closer the score is to 100, the more consistent you are in living up to your brand values. Check how your current image is doing by using these guidelines:

Overall VSP index

0–25   Your overall image is inconsistent with the brand values
          you wish to project. This indicates a great opportunity
          for you to develop all these three elements of your image
          to bring it up to a professional level. Do not be
          disheartened as you may actually be doing well right
          now in your career. What this suggests is that it may not
          be helping to bring you to the future image you want.

26–50   This means that your overall image is fairly inconsistent
          with your brand values, and some areas of your image
          may need more development than others. You need to
          examine which of the indices are contributing to this
          score, and work on closing the gap in your professional
          image.

51–75   You are moderately consistent in matching your overall
          image with your brand values. In some areas you may
          be very consistent and in others fairly inconsistent. It is
          possible that you are highly recognised in one or two
          competencies but some aspects are preventing you from
          achieving a higher level. Examine which of the indices
          are pulling you down, and work on closing this gap to
          reach your aspirations.

76–100   If you have achieved this level, congratulations! It
          means you are consistent in matching your image to your
          brand values in most if not all the areas. You may want
          to ask other people to assess you objectively and see
          if their evaluation is similar to your own. If not, examine
          where there is a gap between your score and theirs to
          see if there are areas you can develop further to bridge
          the gap.

Try This

After you have determined your VSP index, ask 10 other people to evaluate you. To keep it simple, you may ask them to rate you based on their impression of you. For a more representative view, ask a variety of people, e.g. colleagues, boss, staff, vendor, friend or relative. If you want a truthful evaluation from them, give them a self-addressed envelope to return to you anonymously. To get an average score, add up all the indices and divide by the number of people who rated you. Now, take the difference between your self-evaluation and the average of the others' evaluation.

The bigger the difference, the greater the gap between how you perceive yourself and how others perceive you. Examine which areas have the widest gap and work on these areas to close the gap.

How to achieve a higher VSP index

The overall VSP index is a composite measure of your visual, sound and personality impact. To identify and prioritise the areas you want to improve or enhance further, review each individual index to see which aspects you need to focus on to increase your overall score.

Danger Zone

The VSP index is not an examination, so do not be too elated with a high score or depressed with a low one. It is a tool to help you assess yourself — your own perception as well as other people's perception of you. Don't use this tool to evaluate other people if they have not asked you to do so.

Let's examine how each of the individual indices might affect your overall VSP index:

1. **Visual index.**   Identify which aspect of your visual impact needs attention. People look at you as a whole, and if one aspect is visually inconsistent with your professional image, they will judge you as looking unprofessional as a whole. For instance, a woman executive who wears a well-tailored suit to an important business function, but has no makeup on and whose hair looks unkempt, may not come across as looking professional. This means that appearance is more than just about what your wear, and one tiny mismatch could sabotage your whole image.

2. **Sound index.** Similarly, when people judge you on your communication, they are not just listening to what you say, but also how you say it, both verbally and in writing. If your overall index is affected by your sound index, examine which aspect needs more work. Often, these aspects are inter-related, and when we improve one area, the other areas will follow suit. One example has to do with our listening skills: if we pay more attention to what people are saying, we will reduce much miscommunication. In this aspect, it is worth the effort to see how others evaluate you because most of us may think we are great listeners, while other people may see us as completely the opposite.

3. **Personality index.**   Your personality is reflected in your behaviour, and in turn is demonstrated in your relationships with people and the way you handle different situations. While the personality index is not a psychological measure, it does indicate in a broad sense how it is manifested in your behaviour. The extent to which each aspect matches your brand values is also an indication of the behavioural elements that need more focus. It will also be beneficial to examine how others rate you on these areas, so you can tap on your best personality traits to develop a more professional image.

Aha! Moment

The way I behave or conduct myself reflects my personality and this affects my overall image. If I look and sound professional at a business reception, but gobble down the food like there's no tomorrow, it is inconsistent with my brand value to be professional.

I've always known you to be a fast worker, even getting ahead of the buffet line for me — thanks so much.

Make the VSP index work for your professional image

So where does all this fit in your roadmap to success? Let's return to the personal roadmap you charted for yourself in Chapter 2, and write down your VSP index on the spot where you marked where you are. Now, review what your vision is and what your goals are for your future — write down on your destination point the VSP index you wish to achieve by the time you get there. You can treat these two indicators like a highway sign along your roadmap, and if you wish, you can also set targets along the way.

Red, amber or green?

With these targets to improve your VSP index, we can move on to the next chapters to focus on each of the key elements to help you get to your destination. As you take action in each milestone, you can use the VSP index like a traffic sign on your roadmap. If your VSP index is moving up, the light is green for you to move on; if there is no change, the light is amber for you to consider why the results are not showing; if it is lower, the light is red for you to stop and review what went wrong. Take action to get yourself back on track and get on the fast lane.

Red: Stop! Take some time to review your VSP index.

Amber: Hold on. Consider why the results are not showing.

Green: Great work! Time to move on!

Now that you have assessed your VSP index and identified the gaps, we need to take a detailed look at each component in turn. In the next chapter we will go through your visual index by taking a closer look at how you can dress for success.

Star Tips for assessing your professional image:

1. Assess the current status of your professional image using the VSP index. Use this to measure the impact that your visual, sound and personality have on your professional image.

2. Identify how consistent your professional image is with your brand values.

3. Review the VSP index: the closer it is to 100, the more exceptional you are in being consistent with your professional brand values.

4. Focus your attention on each of the key elements that are contributing to a lower score: visual, sound or personality.

5. Compare your self-evaluation with others' perception of you to examine areas where you differ.

6. Focus on areas that could be your blind spots where you rate yourself higher than how others rate you.

7. Write down your VSP index on your roadmap, and indicate what your ideal VSP index is at your destination point.

8. Indicate at each milestone on your roadmap what target you will set for your VSP index when you reach there.

9. Use the next few chapters to take action to improve on your visual, sound or personality impact.

10. Monitor your VSP index regularly to check if you are on the right track.

VISUAL IMPACT: HOW TO DRESS FOR SUCCESS

"If a person is poorly dressed, you notice the clothing. If she is impeccably dressed, you notice the person."

Coco Chanel

4

When I first returned to Singapore from Australia in 1983 after pursuing my Masters degree, I worked as an executive for the national newspaper company in Singapore. The head of my department was someone I admired the minute I met her at the interview. She was impeccably dressed. She had an aura about her that conveyed confidence, power and credibility. At not even 40 years old, she was in a very powerful position, was given a chauffeur-driven company car, and commanded attention everywhere she went. I was just 32 then, and I had a deep desire to be like her but did not really know how.

The first thing I did was to get myself a new work wardrobe, and try to look the part of an executive in a major newspaper company. On a number of occasions my boss would acknowledge that I looked good, and that would make my day. Until one day, she gave me a glance from top to toe, and said, "Nice dress, but wrong shoes." That comment came so unexpectedly that all I could sheepishly offer as an excuse was, "I only have one pair of shoes". It was true, but I felt so small then that my memory has blotted out what happened immediately after that moment.

What I did not forget though was a great lesson on dressing: that to look powerful, you need to be impeccably dressed from top to toe. I was wearing a nice dress, but the sandals I wore with every outfit did not convey a consistent message about who I was. That was why I felt powerless that day.

Power dressing vs powerless dressing

To dress for success, you need some elements of power dressing in your wardrobe. So what makes you look powerful and not powerless?

A general rule-of-thumb is to consider how much skin you are showing: the more skin you show, the more distracting you are, and hence less powerful. This applies to both men and women. Who looks more powerful: a CEO in a jacket suit, or one wearing a figure-hugging dress and plunging neckline? The attention for the former will be on the substance (what's inside) and certainly is more powerful. Now, take a look at your career dressing and check this list to see if you have the elements of power dressing or powerless dressing at work:

Women	Power Dressing	Powerless Dressing
Hair	Short or neatly tied up; well-styled; up-to-date	Long and untidy; not well-maintained; dandruff; out-dated style
Face	Clean and well-maintained skin; shaped eyebrows; appropriate makeup	Poor skin condition; No makeup or too much makeup
Clothes	Skirt suit; pant suit; jacket; pencil skirt; dress pants; knee-length skirt or dress	Spaghetti-strapped blouse; revealing neckline; mini-skirt; figure-hugging dress
Accessories	Classic and elegant styles; high quality and good condition	Faddish styles; broken or damaged; pirated brands
Shoes	Court shoes or pumps; classic style; leather or good quality material	Open-toed sandals; flat shoes; stilettos; sneakers; slippers
Grooming	Clean nails; fresh and pleasant smell	Dirty nails; chipped nail polish; unshaven armpit; bad breath; body odour

Men	Power Dressing	Powerless Dressing
Hair	Short or neatly trimmed; well-styled; up-to-date	Long and untidy; not well-maintained; dandruff; out-dated style
Face	Shaved and clean	Unshaven
Clothes	Jacket suit; shirt and tie; dress trousers; well-maintained	Short-sleeved shirts; collarless T-shirts; stained, torn or wrinkled
Accessories	Classic and elegant styles; high quality and good condition	Faddish styles; broken or damaged; pirated brands
Shoes	Classic leather or good quality material	Sandals; sneakers; slippers
Grooming	Clean nails; fresh and pleasant smell	Dirty nails; bad breath; body odour

 Myth Buster

To look powerful, I need to spend a fortune on branded clothes, expensive jewellery and several pairs of leather shoes.

If this were true, then only the rich could look powerful. If you are discerning about good quality, you will know that clothes need not be branded or expensive. While you may pay a little more for better-quality clothes or accessories, they also last longer and in the end save you money.

Aha! Moment

Power dressing is not just for top executives. If I want people to trust, like or admire me, I need to convey power.

Three elements of professional style

You may notice from the examples given that power dressing is not about having dominance over another person. Power can have many meanings, and there are many different forms of power. In the case of power dressing, we not only want to convey authority, but also respect, confidence, credibility, trust, interest and likeability. It is not just dictatorial power but also an element of personal power that draws people to us.

The extent to which we convey power in our dressing is determined by how we use these three elements in our dress style:

Authority

Approachability

Individuality

Think of each of these elements as a sliding scale (1 to 10) and the way you put your dressing together depends on how much of each element you wish to convey at work.

Authority

If we look at the dressing of uniformed personnel like policemen and military officers, we would give them a high score on the authority scale. I have brothers who served in the military in Singapore (it is compulsory for all men to enlist when they turn 18). Their uniforms had to be starched and well pressed, and their leather boots had to be polished until they were so shiny they could see their own reflection in them. If you meet a scruffy-looking uniformed man in public, you would most likely take a few points off his authority scale. The higher the rank, the more authority is conveyed in the uniforms.

Fast Fact

A high-quality jacket projects an authoritative and powerful image. It is worth your investment to have at least one in your professional wardrobe.

The same goes with our professional dressing. Now consider your position, role and responsibility, and determine how much authority you need to convey at work. Some professions and positions like lawyers, teachers and senior management would need to reflect stronger authority. Other professions or positions like accountants, managers and consultants may require medium authority. If you have no one reporting to you at work and if you are not involved in decision-making, you will most likely be lower on the authority scale. Using this scale, indicate with a cross (x) how much authority you wish to convey at work:

| 1 | 2 | 3 | 4 | 5 | 6 | 7 | 8 | 9 | 10 |

LOW   MEDIUM   HIGH

Approachability

If your work requires you to build relationships, either with customers or colleagues, and the company's business relies on your interaction with customers or employees to grow, you will need to convey a higher degree of approachability. A pre-school teacher may wish to convey more approachability than, say, a high school teacher. An insurance sales person needs to be very approachable to attract customers. A traffic cop, on the other hand, may not want to look too approachable (which may explain why they wear dark glasses when giving you a ticket).

Based on the work you do and how important relationship-building affects your company, indicate with a cross (x) how much approachability you wish to convey at work:

| 1 | 2 | 3 | 4 | 5 | 6 | 7 | 8 | 9 | 10 |

LOW   MEDIUM   HIGH

Fast Fact

Informal and casual wear generally conveys an approachable image. If you need to look formal and yet approachable, you can add softer colours and fabrics.

Individuality

Remember when we talked about your personal brand values, I mentioned that each of us is unique and there is the special something that makes us different? While our work may determine how much authority or approachability we need to convey, there is also an element of how much individuality can be incorporated into our professional dressing. With uniformed personnel, there is very little room for individuality in style. In the creative industry, there is a lot of room to incorporate your individual style.

Review your brand values and see if you need to convey some element of individuality in your professional style. For example, if you are *creative* or *progressive*, you need to convey a higher level of individuality in your style. On the other hand, if your brand value is *traditional* and *dependable*, you may convey a lower level of individuality. Again, indicate with a cross (x) how much individuality you wish to convey at work

LOW   MEDIUM   HIGH

Fast Fact

Any creative element in your dressing adds a touch of individuality. This could include a different cut in the garment, a mix of patterns, a contrast of colours, or a piece of statement jewellery.

Dress for your future career

The exercise you have just completed provides a basis to help you decide if your current style is helping you to achieve your future career goals. It's important that you don't just dress for your present career, as your style will let people know where you are going — down, up, or not going anywhere.

Here is a guide to help you identify the elements you need to incorporate into your professional style for your future career. This is neither an exhaustive nor mutually exclusive list, as you need to adapt to the organisation, industry or culture you work in.

	Low	Medium	High

Authority	Junior officer
	Admin assistant
	Junior secretary
	Sales rep
	Customer service
	  rep
		Manager and
		  executive
		Teacher
		Executive secretary
		Trainer
		Accountant
		Financial planner
			Chairman
			CEO
			Senior management
			Lawyer
			Chief engineer
			School principal
			Banker

Approachability	Chairman
	CEO
	CFO
	Engineer
	Lawyer
	Scientist
	Lab technician
	Auditor
		Mid- to senior
		  manager
		Secretary
		High-school
		  teacher
		Coach
		Counsellor
			Receptionist
			Sales rep
			Customer service
			  rep
			Real estate agent
			Financial planner
			Pre-school teacher

Individuality	Lawyer
	Teacher
	Accountant
	Engineer
	IT professional
	Researcher
		Mid-to senior
		  manager
		Broadcast journalist
		Art teacher
			Designer
			Architect
			Hairdresser
			Advertising
			  and marketing
			  executive
			Fashion editor
			Actor

Putting your professional style together

Now that you have determined the extent to which you need to project authority, approachability and individuality, we can start to put your professional style together. If you need to project a high level of authority at work, your professional style should be more formal and classic. If you need to be very approachable, your professional style can be smart and relaxed. If you want to project a high degree of individuality, you can add a creative look to your professional style. You can incorporate each of the three elements in your dressing according to what will help you to achieve your goals.

In this next chart we look at the elements you need to create the visual impact you desire. Depending on the situation, you may decide to reflect only one element or some aspects of each element. For example, if you are a keynote speaker, regardless of your position, you may need to reflect a higher authority with medium approachability. If you are female, you may select a red tailored jacket over a laced camisole, teamed with a pair of black pants. You could also go for a pair of shoes with three-inch heels to up the authority scale. If you are male and need to raise the approachability factor, you may go for a different colour jacket and pants. You can decide how much of each element you wish to incorporate and where. It's really up to you.

ELEMENTS OF PROFESSIONAL STYLE FOR WOMEN

	Low	**Medium**	**High**
Authority	*Informal sweater instead of jacket:* Short-sleeve blouse Frills, pleats, gathers Prints Flowing dress Costume accessories Close-toed flats	*Separates with blazer or light jacket as an option:* Shirt blouse or with collar and sleeves A-line or pleated skirt Smart pants Shirt dress Quality accessories Low heels	*Tailored and formal wear:* Skirt suit with shirt blouse Pencil skirt Jacket over sheath dress Classic accessories Court shoes or pumps
Approachability	*Top is more formal and bottom informal:* Blazer over lace blouse Sweater over flowing dress Minimal accessories Low heels	*No jacket with some formal elements:* Blouse over smart pants Subtle prints Moderate details and accessories Close-toed flats	*No jacket:* Print blouse and flowing skirt Softer fabrics and prints Frills, lace in tops Pleated or gathered skirts More accessories Peep-toed shoes
Individuality	*Follow dress code and add where allowed:* Subtle colours Simple prints Simple accessories	*Some creative elements in top or bottom:* Dressy trousers Statement jewellery Funky bag or shoes	*Creative wear from top to bottom:* Mix prints (e.g. floral with stripes) Contrast colours (e.g. purple and orange) Quirky accessories Trendy shoes

ELEMENTS OF PROFESSIONAL STYLE FOR MEN

	Low	**Medium**	**High**
Authority	*No jacket, no tie:* Shirt and pants Short-sleeved shirt Check shirt Chino pants Loafer shoes	*Tailored shirt and pants with optional jacket:* Long-sleeved shirt Striped shirt Patterned tie (stripes or foulard) Quality belt and shoes	*Tailored and formal wear:* Jacket suit Dress shirt and pants; Classic silk tie Quality belt Leather laced-up shoes
Approachability	*Optional jacket or blazer:* Shirt and pants No prints Dress pants Laced-up shoes	*No jacket with optional tie:* Subtle prints Smart pants Plain accessories Slip-on shoes	*No jacket, no tie:* Print shirt Chino pants More colour More accessories Loafers
Individuality	*Follow dress code and add where allowed:* Subtle colours No prints Conventional accessories Slip-on shoes	*Some creative elements in top or bottom:* Blazer with designs Fun tie Silk pants Funky belt Loafer shoes	*Creative wear from top to bottom:* Mix prints (e.g. striped shirt with floral tie) Contrast colours (e.g. purple and orange stripes) Quirky accessories Boots

Danger Zone

If your office environment is very casual, do not fall into the trap of dressing down when you need to reflect higher authority. For example, if you are making a sales presentation, you must put on a jacket even if your audience does not. If you also need to look approachable, you may wear separates rather than suits, and remove the jacket after the presentation.

Match your professional style to your situation

No one walks around with a sign on his or her forehead that says, "I am a lawyer" or "I help you build wealth". When people need to make decisions about you, whether it is to hire you, promote you, or buy from you, they look for signs in your visual appearance. This is where the three elements of authority, approachability and individuality come in: when people see your formal business wear, they are reading a sign that says, "I am in charge". When they see you in casual wear, they are reading, "I am relaxed and just want to have fun."

While you now have a clear idea of how much authority, approachability or individuality you need to project on a day-to-day basis, there are times when you need to tweak each element to suit the situation. When I was working in the market research industry, most researchers conveyed medium authority, low approachability and low individuality in their dressing. This made sense as they didn't see clients every day. However, when there was an important client presentation to make, there was a shift in the authority scale by the addition of a jacket. On Fridays, when we were allowed to dress casually, the approachability scale went up. The men could leave their ties at home, and the women could swap their heels for flats. The exception was if they had to meet clients.

There are variations in what is considered acceptable office wear in different industries, cultures and environments. It's important to take all of these into consideration when you decide what to wear on a particular occasion. To make the right choice, you need to have a wardrobe that can allow you to pull the appropriate elements together. Let's now take a look at how you can put your wardrobe together.

Creating a professional wardrobe without spending a fortune

How often do you stare at your wardrobe full of clothes and lament, "*I have nothing to wear*"? How many times have you put something on and then made several changes before deciding on what to wear? Don't worry, it happens to us all. The solution is to create a wardrobe using the *capsule* principle.

Think of a capsule as a solution to your wardrobe woes — it has all the right ingredients that will work for any specific problem.

What you need in your wardrobe are capsules for different occasions, or 'stories' you want to tell. Each capsule is a group of clothing items (including accessories) that can mix and match to tell one story about you. Depending on the situation, you may pull together different items to project more authority, approachability or individuality. Once you have this basic wardrobe, you can then expand on a particular capsule or create entirely new ones.

So how do we start building a capsule?

To start creating a capsule, you need to decide what the story is based on your three brand values. Then select the clothing items you need on the basis of these three things:

1. A colour scheme that matches the story

2. Styles that work together

3. Fabrics that are compatible

Let's use the example of a sales engineer who has the brand values of credibility, enthusiasm and empathy. His professional style needs to project high authority as well as approachability, and a small degree of individuality. One basic capsule he needs is shown here:

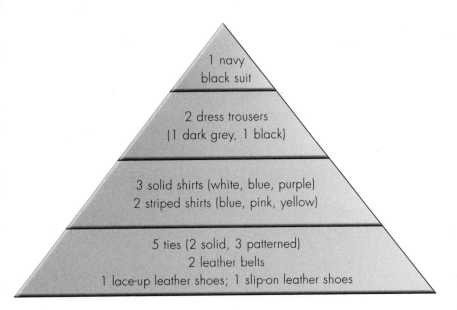

On a day when he is making a sales presentation, he needs the navy black suit and white shirt to look credible (high authority). At the same time, he also needs to look enthusiastic and empathetic (high approachability), so he could select a patterned tie with approachable colours like yellow and blue. To add a touch of individuality, he could wear a trendy watch in black and silver. On other days when he is not meeting clients and wants to raise his individuality factor, he could go with the purple shirt and yellow tie.

Try This

How many different outfits can you create from this capsule (for women)?

   1 black jacket

   1 red sweater

   2 skirts (1 black, 1 dark grey)

   1 black pants

   1 red/black dress

   3 blouses (1 white, floral red/black, 1 mustard yellow)

   1 black camisole

How many different outfits can you create from this capsule (for men)?

   1 black jacket

   1 grey black blazer

   3 pants (1 black, 1 grey, 1 dark grey)

   3 shirts (1 white, 1 lilac, 1 striped blue/white)

   3 matching ties for each shirt

Check your answers at the end of this chapter.

You can see how, by changing one item in the capsule, it's possible to tell a slightly different story. Remember, if you are to maximise every item in your capsule, it needs to go with at least three other items. For example, the yellow-striped shirt can go with the navy black suit, dark grey pants and black pants (that makes three outfits). Next, add a blue tie to each of these, and you now have six outfits. See how many different outfits you can put together from this capsule to tell a special story each day.

Five steps to a wardrobe makeover

Now that we've analysed the theory of wardrobe planning and done the number-crunching, it's time to go to your wardrobe and take the next step: clearing the dead wood and creating a professional wardrobe.

1. Divide all the items into two piles: one for all items you have not worn for the past 12 months or so; the other for items you wear regularly.

2. Go through the first pile and ask yourself of each item: can you part with it? If yes, pack it in a box for charity or the recycle bin. If no, decide if you must keep it for sentimental reasons. If not, get rid of it.

3. Go through the second pile and put items that belong together in a capsule. Any single item that does not go with three other items is in a capsule of its own.

4. Go through each capsule to see if they project your professional style. Remove items that do not convey power, i.e. authority, approachability or individuality (this includes faded or damaged items).

5. Review the remaining capsules and make a shopping list of items you may need to complete each capsule.

Before you make a dash for the shopping mall, we now need to look at whether the colours in your existing capsule are working for you. While you may have complementary colours in your capsule, we want to be sure they are the right colours for you. If not, there could be a lot more shopping to do!

Star Tips for creating a professional style

1. Invest in a high quality jacket to convey authority in your professional image.

2. Use softer colours or fabrics to project approachability.

3. Mix patterns and colours to give a touch of individuality in your professional style.

4. Dress for your future career by incorporating the relevant elements in your professional wardrobe.

5. Match your professional style to the situation, industry or culture.

6. Create your professional wardrobe using the capsule principle.

7. Build a capsule based on the story you wish to tell about your professional image.

8. Select items for each capsule based on colours, style and fabrics that tell the same story.

9. Ensure every item in the capsule goes with three other items.

10. Take action now to give your wardrobe a makeover.

Answer to Try This on page 64: You can create at least 30 outfits with the women's capsule and 35 with the men's capsule.

COLOUR DIRECTIONS FOR DIFFERENT PROFESSIONS

"Mere colour, unspoiled by meaning, and unallied with definite form, can speak to the soul in a thousand different ways."

Oscar Wilde

5

As I am writing this book in my office, looking out of the window, I see a tree swaying in the breeze and I feel peaceful and calm. I know it is a blazing hot day as the sun's rays beam through the window of my air-conditioned office. Yet, why do I feel the serenity and calmness not usually derived from a hot and humid day in Singapore? It is just a plain tree but it is full of green leaves. What if the leaves were black, I wondered? Would I feel differently? Most likely I would. Thank God trees are not black!

That's the magic of colour: it can convey feelings, emotions, and intentions without us saying a word. Colour can reflect position, status and power too. Colour can attract and deflect attention. You can use colour to create the impact you want. In this chapter, we will look at how colour affects your professional image and how you can select the right colours to make your image work for you.

The significance of colour

Colour is nature's gift. It plays a significant part in all societies, cultures and ways of life. We make decisions about colours all the time, whether consciously or subconsciously. A bridal dress is usually expected to be white and not black, unless the bride is marrying into a gothic group or trying to make a statement about her individuality. From the time an expectant mother knows the gender of her baby, she usually starts decorating the room with gender specific colours: pink for a girl or blue for a boy. Try the opposite when you buy a gift for a baby and see if you get some rude stares. However, colours may have different meanings in different cultures. For example, red is an auspicious colour for the Chinese, but a colour of mourning in South Africa. So be aware of the meaning of different colours in your workplace and culture so that you create the appropriate impact.

The impact of colour

Colour is one of the first things people notice about your clothes. They may not be aware of this, and may think you look friendly or cold, energetic or dull, and will act accordingly based on this perception. The colour you are wearing may have something to do with it.

At school reunion dinners, you may hear comments like, "You look the same after all these years," or "Have you been on a diet?" Before you take it as an insult or a compliment, you may want to assess whether the colours you wear to school reunion dinners flatter or sabotage you.

Fast Fact

When you wear the right colours, you look younger, fresher, and healthier, and the focus of attention is on you, not the colours.

When it comes to professional dressing, you want people to notice you, hire you, buy from you and continue to work with you or conduct business with you. The right colours can make us attract the right people in our work, so it's important to enhance and flatter our best features, and hide the 'flaws'. So how do colours help us create a greater impact on our professional appearance? Let's look at what colours can do to you:

• **Dark colours.** Any colour that has black added to it makes it darker. The more black we add, the darker it is. Black recedes and makes everything look smaller. Hence, the darker the colour, the smaller things will appear. It goes without saying that black or darker colours make you look slimmer and smaller. So wear these colours in areas where you wish to look slimmer, but not if you already look like Olive in the cartoon *Popeye*. If you wish to attract more attention, avoid a full black outfit or you may be mistaken as a bouncer who is usually in black shirt, tie and pants. Many service staff are dressed in all-black, as they are not supposed to be noticed. (Maybe this is why you sometimes cannot find service staff when you need them?)

- **Light colours.** White or water lightens a colour. This produces pastel colours like pink and baby blue, or washed colours that are in contrast to colours with black added to them. White or lighter colours tend to make everything look larger. The lighter the colour, the larger things will appear. So if you get a comment that you may have put on weight, perhaps you are wearing white or light colours in areas that make you look bigger than you already are. Avoid lighter colours if you do not wish to draw attention to certain parts of your body, especially the bottom.

 Danger Zone

The chest, waist, hip and thighs are danger zones for white or lighter colours if they are relatively big. If you do not wish to look larger than you already are in these areas, avoid white or solid pastels there.

- **Bright colours.** All primary colours, which have not been darkened or lightened, are bright. Many people mistake bright colours to be red, yellow or orange only. However, blue, green and purple can also be bright. Fabrics can be made to look brighter if they are shiny or have glitter. All bright colours attract attention and look larger. If you need more attention, but do not wish to look any larger, you may choose a brighter colour at an appropriate place (e.g. a brooch or a tie). There are also varying degrees of brightness, and you need to match this to your skin tone so you do not wear a colour that is brighter than your skin.

- **Muted colours.** All colours that have been toned down, either by adding a duller colour like grey or brown, or contrasting colour like green and red, become muted. This is the opposite of bright although there can also be variations of mutedness. Think of colours like mustard yellow, khaki green, or salmon pink. Muted colours minimise attention and seem lighter. The more muted the colour, the softer the look, and the more you fade into the background. If you do not have a bright complexion, keep to more muted colours so that you can get the right kind of attention.

Fast Fact

When you wear colours that are brighter than your complexion, people notice the colours and not you. When you wear colours that are duller than your complexion, they may not even notice you.

The messages of colour

Colour affects not only your overall physical appearance but it can also send different messages about you. Let's now look at how you can look professional by wearing the right colours. Bear in mind that these meanings are universally applied to the business world, but you may need to adjust accordingly when you are in a different cultural or social setting.

- **Black.** A serious, formal and conservative colour. Men in black suits usually represent supreme authority, e.g. president, CEO, lawyer, etc. Women in black suits are considered authoritative and therefore less approachable. If the black suit is teamed with a colourful blouse or accessory, it tones down the seriousness.

  When to wear: It is appropriate to wear black when you are interviewing for a top job, making a presentation, attending a formal business meeting or conference, holding a senior position, or working in a professional services firm. Many service personnel wear black, which shows their seriousness in serving customers.

  When to avoid: If you know your boss does not wear a black suit, you should avoid this colour, especially when attending a business meeting with him. You may send the wrong message that you are in charge. In this case, you could mix your black with other colours or go for grey or navy black.

Myth Buster

Black is the safest colour to wear at the office, and I will look professional in black at all times.

Although black is the most common colour for formal suits and jackets, it may not always work for your professional image if the messages you want to send are approachability and individuality.

- **White.** A pure, innocent and youthful colour. This is opposite to black and does not convey power or status in business. Hospitals use white uniforms to represent sterility and cleanliness. Men in business wear white shirts to present a sharp and smart image, and will always team it with a dark jacket or tie to create the power look. A woman in a white dress or suit conveys softness and, at the same time, can be seen as tidy and meticulous.

  When to wear: If you work in an environment that represents cleanliness and sterility, wearing white can assure people you are the right person for the job. White shirts for men are suitable for office wear, but not white pants. Women can wear white with other colours, but you must bear in mind that white always makes you appear larger.

  When to avoid: If you need to look authoritative and powerful, white does not help. In some cultures, men in white pants are seen to be playful so it's best to avoid this in business. White gets dirty easily so avoid this colour when entertaining for business, as any spills on a white shirt or blouse will not wash off easily.

- **Blue.** A trustworthy, loyal and conservative colour. All shades of blue convey a calming effect and are more approachable than black. Navy blue is thus a good alternative colour to black in business, as it conveys authority and at the same time it's not as serious.

  When to wear: Suitable for everyday business wear. It is also appropriate for any job interview or during a job appraisal for a promotion. Navy blue is also a suitable basic colour that can be dressed up or down to look more authoritative or approachable.

  When to avoid: If you need to stand out and be noticed more, or to show your creativity, avoid this colour. However, you can select a brighter blue, provided it is not brighter than your complexion.

- **Red.** An exciting, energetic and stimulating colour. This colour sends a message of power in a different way from black. Red conveys a high energy, unlike black, which conveys a solemn energy. A man in a black suit and red tie creates a very powerful and energetic message. A woman in a red jacket is seen to be powerful and inspiring.

When to wear: If you are in charge and need to convey authority and motivate the team, add some red to your outfit. If you are the guest-of-honour, speaker or presenter at an important event, wear red to stand out from the crowd.

When to avoid: Stay away from this colour at a job appraisal with your boss, unless you are about to take over her job. It is also not advisable to wear red when you are going into a potentially conflicting situation, like a union meeting. Avoid this colour if your work requires you to instill discipline or calm, e.g. in a school, psychiatric ward or hospital. Red is also a sexy colour, so wear this colour in an appropriate style so as not to send the wrong messages at work.

Avoid wearing red when going into a meeting where there may potentially be conflict.

- **Yellow.** A cheerful, fun and optimistic colour. Yellow attracts attention but if too bright can be overwhelming for the eye. Like red, yellow can generate high energy as well, but in a more friendly way. A man in a yellow tie will make you smile. A woman in a yellow blouse will set a positive tone at a team meeting.

  When to wear: On days when team morale needs to be boosted, or you are working on a team project. It is also good for networking events as you will attract attention and at the same time look friendly and approachable. Yellow is not an easy colour to wear, so use this colour in the right tone and shade and in appropriate amounts in your clothing so it is not too overpowering.

  When to avoid: As this colour, like red, creates high energy, it is also not suitable for negotiations and conflict resolution meetings. The brighter the yellow, the higher the energy. In some cultures, yellow is reserved for the sacred and imperial family, so avoid this colour if you are not one of them.

- **Green.** A peaceful, serene and steady colour. Green is universally associated with nature and a healthy environment. It soothes, calms and evokes a healing effect, which could explain why surgeons wear green. Since it is not seen to be an assertive colour, green is seldom used in formal business wear. Consequently, green is good for creating harmony with colleagues or clients, rather than for winning that million-dollar deal.

  When to wear: This is a very good colour to wear for conflict resolutions and difficult negotiations. Green can help calm nerves and release tension. Try adding some green in your outfit when you are counselling or coaching someone on their work performance.

  When to avoid: If you need to be the focus of attention, this colour may not work for you. As a presenter, you may put the audience to sleep if you are wearing green. Go for a bright or lime green instead to create a harmonious relationship and at the same time, attract attention.

- **Purple.** A grand, royal and luxurious colour. This is a rare colour in nature, hence its association with royalty. As such, it can also convey authority, power and status. Men in purple shirts or ties can look special, and women in purple can look sophisticated.

  When to wear: When you need to impress people, or on a special occasion, purple can be very effective. If your work requires you to create high visibility or have a high public profile, a touch of purple can make you look important. If you want to project creativity, you can also inject some purple in your outfit.

  When to avoid: Purple works the opposite of green for negotiations and conflict resolutions. Given its association with power and authority, it can convey a message of arrogance, and so may not be effective for creating harmony. It may not be so effective in counselling and coaching situations.

 Fast Fact

In ancient days, purple dye was made from the mucous glands of a snail. It required thousands of snails to make one gram of dye, making it a colour that only royalty could afford. This is why purple is still considered a grand and luxurious colour today.

Colours for your professional image

Now that you understand the significance and impact of colour, and the messages you are sending through the colours you wear, let's take a look at how colour can help you in projecting your professional image in a powerful way.

Let's return to your wardrobe, which hopefully has been rid of items that you cannot use and that are incongruent with your professional image. If you have not done so, go back to Chapter 4 and return to this page after your wardrobe review.

For each capsule you have put together, note the colour scheme. What are the common colours in each capsule? Review the messages you are sending through these colours. Are they reflecting your brand values? Do they project your past, current or future image? What new colours can you add to help you send messages to advance your career?

If you do not find any colour scheme, and you have a wide range of colours, you may be sending very mixed messages. Review the messages you wish to convey and set aside the colours that can help you do this. For the remaining items, consider removing them from your wardrobe if they are not working for your professional image.

Hopefully, you still have some clothes left after this exercise. If not, you can start building a new wardrobe from here! Most likely, you will still have a decent set of clothes to wear for the coming week, and can start planning to build on this wardrobe. Based on the three elements of professional style, and your personal brand values, select what new colours you could introduce to your new wardrobe. Here are some suggestions to guide you.

Authority	Black, Navy Black, Blue, Red, Purple, and dark colours
Approachability	White, Brown, Green, Yellow, Orange, Pink, and light colours
Individuality	Purple, Fuchsia, contrasting and bright colours

Try This

To test the impact of colours, try to put together an outfit to represent authority, approachability and individuality. Then go to the streets and ask a stranger for directions. Note what style and colours you are wearing to get the friendliest response. Or, walk into a high-end boutique and observe the kind of service you receive in each of the three different outfits.

Determining your personal colouring

When you have decided on the colours for your professional image, you will need to take one last step to get a personalised colour analysis done by a certified image professional. While everyone can wear all colours, we need to determine the tones and shades that best suit our skin tone. Even basic colours like black and blue come in different tones and shades, and some of us look better in pure black while others may look better in brown black.

It is beyond the scope of this book to provide a detailed personal colour analysis, so it's best for you to consider investing in a reputable image consultant if you would like to ensure your colours work best for you. At the same time, you can also have a personal style analysis done to determine the garment styles that suit your body shape.

Once you know your colour directions and what styles suit your body shape, and armed with your shopping list, you can hit the malls and get that image makeover!

Star Tips for making colours work for you

1. Wear darker colours to look smaller and less noticeable; wear lighter colours to look bigger and draw attention.

2. Wear brighter colours to draw attention and muted colours to minimise attention.

3. Select the right colours to create the professional impact you want.

4. Choose black for a more authoritative colour in business; choose navy blue to look trustworthy and approachable at the same time.

5. Add some red to your outfit if you need to create attention or convey more power.

6. Use some green to create a harmonious relationship at the workplace.

7. Look unique and sophisticated by including some purple in your outfit.

8. Review your brand values and select the colours that convey your professional image effectively.

9. Review your wardrobe and select the colours that convey the three elements of professional dressing.

10. Engage a certified image professional to analyse your personal colour and style so you will wear the colours in the right shades and tones for your skin.

THE SOUNDS OF SUCCESS

"Let your speech be always with grace, seasoned with salt, that you may know how to answer every man."

Colossians 4:6

In my childhood days, before the invention of the television, my mother would have the *Redifusion* on all day. It was Singapore's first commercial and cable-transmitted radio station, and our main source of family entertainment on evenings and weekends. My mother got us hooked on Cantonese dramas, and our favourite storyteller was Lei Dai Sor who kept us spellbound with his voice. We would always be home in time for dinner because Lei Dai Sor would come on right afterwards.

I also had my own favourite English-speaking DJ, and would switch to the station just to listen to his voice. He had a rich, powerful and captivating voice. I imagined he would be dashing and handsome, and I secretly wished to meet and fall in love with him one day! The day arrived, 20 years later, when I attended a company dinner and dance where he was the MC. To my disappointment, he was a far cry from the dream man in my imagination. His voice was still fabulous, but I wished he had stayed behind the *Redifusion* box.

This was indeed an eye-opener for me on how important and powerful the human voice can be. When people can't see you when you speak, be it on the phone, Skype or audio recording, the impression they form is based solely on the messages you send through your voice. When people meet you in person, their first impression will be based not just on your looks, but also how you come across when you speak. In this chapter, we will look at how you can polish the sound of your brand and send the right messages about your professional image through your voice.

 Aha! Moment

When I look professional, people expect me to sound professional too. I need to project the same messages through my appearance and the way I speak.

Sounding professional

When you speak, your voice sends signals and you conjure up images in people's heads. This is why storytelling is so powerful and, in my childhood days, it did not require visuals to be effective. We could imagine how evil a villain looked, and how frightening a ghost was just by listening to the way the story was told. Similarly, when you speak, people can imagine things, not just through the words you use, but also by listening to the sound and tone of your voice. If it sounds positive and energetic, people imagine you to be a positive and energetic person. If it sounds angry, people imagine you with clenched fists and teeth, and will tend to react negatively.

So how does your brand sound?

Are you sending the key messages about who you are when you communicate? This includes verbal, written and non-verbal communication. It involves not only the language or words you use, but also how they are put together and the way they are delivered. Let's return to the VSP index you completed in Chapter 3, and look at the assessment of your communication.

If the score on your Sound index is not consistent with your brand values, identify which aspects of your communication needs more work. Compare the differences in your personal evaluation and others to find out which aspects need to project a more positive message.

Next, review the three brand attributes you came up with in Chapter 2, and evaluate how you sound on each of these communication areas, and what you need to work on to sound more like your brand values. You may evaluate yourself or ask your friends and colleagues to evaluate you. In the example below, if your brand values are efficient, credible and inspiring, your evaluation may look like this:

	I sound...	**To be efficient, credible and inspiring, I need to sound more...**
Verbal	Friendly and casual	Confident and knowledgeable
Written	Fluent but long-winded	Precise and clear
Listening	Patient and caring	Understanding
Presentations	Nervous and boring	Articulate, energetic and persuasive
Non-verbal	Poised and calm	Polished

Focus on areas where you need more work to project your brand values effectively. This could involve the quality of your voice, your language, or the approach or technique you use. Where you feel personal coaching or training is needed, sign up for a course to tackle the specific area. For our purpose here, we will look at enhancing the verbal aspect of your professional sound.

The quality of your voice

In my past career in research, I used to conduct focus group discussions and have everything recorded. I used to hate hearing my voice on tape. It just didn't sound like what I heard when I was speaking. My colleagues would assure me it sounded exactly like my voice, and according to them it did not irritate them as it did me. I still didn't like my voice on tape until one day I was given the role of 'announcer' at a huge public fair. My colleagues would come to the reception area where I was seated and ask, "Who's the announcer with that professional voice?" From that day onwards, I learnt to love my voice.

Fast Fact

When you speak, the voice you hear sounds different from what others are hearing. The reason for this is that we hear ourselves like *sensurround*, as the voice we hear bounces around inside us creating the stereo effect. This is absent when it gets projected to others, so it's no wonder we don't like the sound of our voice on audio recordings! However, this is the voice that people hear, so you'd better get used to it, and do the best you can with what nature has given you.

Each of us has a unique voice, and this makes us special. No matter how much you hate your voice, you cannot trade it with someone else. However, you can train your voice to enhance its quality and make it work for you. There are two key aspects to voice quality:

Technical quality

Dramatic quality

- **Technical quality.** This has to do with the pitch, volume, speed and range which, when combined, makes the voice sound interesting or boring.

- **Dramatic quality.** This has to do with where we place an emphasis, pause, add emotion, or variety in our technical delivery. This establishes a connection with the listener.

We can train both the technical and dramatic quality of our voices, and this requires discipline and daily practice. Let's look at how you can develop each of these aspects to enhance the quality of your voice and help you sound professional.

 Myth Buster

There's nothing I can do about my voice since I am born with it.

Not so! With practice and discipline, you can train your voice to work for you. Look for the special quality in your voice: is it a high pitch or husky tone? Find how far a range you can stretch, from the lowest of the range to the highest of your pitch. Work on the range so you can speak at the lowest when you start and go higher when you need to.

Enhancing the technical quality

The best test of whether we have a good voice quality is when we know we are understood, and we get positive response when we speak. Ask yourself these key questions:

- Do people often ask you to repeat yourself?

- Do you find people not paying attention when you speak?

- Do you sound monotonous?

- Do you find that you are frequently misunderstood?

If your answer is yes to most of these questions, it's time to examine whether your technical quality has anything to do with it. Review each of these elements and see what needs changing.

- **Pitch.** This can be too low, too high or just right. A lower pitch is the most pleasant and powerful, as it comes across as being steady and rich. When you start with a lower pitch, it allows you to go higher without screeching. A high pitch is usually associated with excitement and tense situations, and it is very uncomfortable to listen to someone speaking constantly at a high pitch. To project a professional image, always speak with a low to medium pitch, and only go high when emphasising certain points.

 Try This

When working on your voice, and to hear what others are hearing, cup your hands behind your ears as you speak. If, for example, you think you have a high-pitched voice, you will hear how high it is when you try this exercise. You can then work to bring your pitch down to a level that is less jarring.

- **Volume.** This can be too soft or too loud, depending on how many people you are speaking to. There is no instrument for you to adjust your volume, so you need to decide on the most comfortable level for people to hear you clearly. Always speak loud enough for the person standing furthest away from you to hear you. When making a presentation, speak loud enough for the people in the back row. If you speak too softly, people will think you lack confidence or have no substance. If you speak too loudly, you may appear domineering and overpowering.

Danger Zone

When speaking on the phone, speak as if the person is standing in front of you, not miles away. Thanks to technology, you don't need to increase your volume even if they are overseas. When you speak too loudly on the phone, people might think you are shouting, or just being unprofessional, especially when talking about business.

- **Speed.** The danger here is to speak too slowly or quickly. The best speed is at a conversational level, like how broadcasters read the news. They do not read word for word as it appears on their prompt cards, but they sound more conversational. If you are thinking as you speak, you are too slow. If you are interrupted often, or if people try to help you with the next word, it could be a sign that you are speaking too slowly. If you speak too quickly people do not have a chance to reflect on what you are saying, and this may result in endless arguments about what you said and what you meant.

- **Range.** This has to do with the tones, like notes in music. When you use the same tone throughout your speech, you will sound monotonous. It is like someone who is tone-deaf and sings in one note throughout the song. If you put people to sleep during a presentation despite having very rich content, it could be a sign that you sound monotonous.

The most interesting voice is one that covers a range of notes that makes your speech come alive. You can also add variety by raising the dramatic effect in your voice.

Enhancing the dramatic quality

Everyone loves to listen to a story. If you have ever listened to a presenter telling a story, you know how cleverly they get their point across and grab the attention of their audience. The story sounds interesting when we are expressive while telling a story. The dramatic effects help the listener to visualise what is being described, and to internalise the point being made. If you want to be more persuasive or connect better with people when you speak, look at how you can enhance the dramatic quality in your voice.

Here are some examples of how you can enhance your dramatic quality:

- **Emphasis.** Placing emphasis on a word drives home the message in a more powerful way, and tells people what you really mean. You can use pitch, volume or speed to make an emphasis and create the effect you want. Take the sentence, "I am delighted to see you." Now consider where you could place emphasis by changing your pitch, volume or speed. If you emphasise the word 'delighted', you could raise your pitch and volume slightly on the second syllable 'de-lighted', and pause slightly before 'to see you'.

- **Emotion.**   While the words you use are important in conveying your meaning, the emotion you put into them makes it crystal clear. Misunderstanding can arise not because of what was said, but how it was said. This is sometimes referred to as tone, which occurs when we put different emotions into a word or phrase. If you want to connect more with people when you speak, learn to put more feeling in your words. You can change the meaning of words by changing your emotion. Children are really natural at this, as you can tell when they have done something naughty and apologise sincerely. If they know you will forgive them anyway, they put on a cheeky smile and say it in a light-hearted tone.

 Try This

See how you can change the meaning of the following paragraph by reading it three times with these different emotions:

Enthusiasm
Anger
Indifference

"The Internet can do anything these days. You have heard of the sound blaster; soon you will get the 'smell-blaster', which allows you to receive not just data, images and sound, but also smell. Imagine you will be able to click on your computer one day to choose (and smell) a perfume for your loved one before buying it. Or, better still, you can smell the gunfire and explosives during a computer game. That's the future of the Internet."

- **Pause.** An intended pause can dramatically change the power of your message. Silence is indeed golden when you pause to grab attention, to make a point, to transition to the next point, or to invite a response. Powerful people know how and when to use a pause when they speak. It helps to moderate your speed and emphasise a point. It helps you to assess if the audience is with you or drifting away. Using pauses effectively is a powerful way to connect with your listener.

 Try This

> To learn how to use pauses more effectively, try reading a newspaper or magazine article to a friend or colleague. Use a marker to highlight where you will pause to emphasise a point, create an impact or get a response. First, read it without pausing except at full stops. Then, try pausing at the highlighted words and see how you can create the impact you desire.

The 3 C's of sounding professional

Whatever profession you are in, whatever position, and no matter who you are dealing with, these 3 C's are taken into consideration when you speak:

Confidence

Credibility

Convincing

Whether you are speaking on the phone, or in person, you must sound *confident* to get attention. Whether you are providing information or explaining an action, you must sound *credible*. Whether you are selling a product or making a point in an argument, you must sound *convincing*. Let's look at how you can use the technical and dramatic qualities to sound more confident, credible and convincing.

To sound confident:

- Start with your lowest pitch, and move up when you need to stress a word.

- Speak loud enough for all to hear you. At this volume, you can still be heard when you go softer to create suspense; or louder to create excitement.

- Speak at a slow to moderate pace with pauses at the right points. Increase your speed when you need to create interest.

- Use strong, stable and positive emotions. This is not the time to be over-dramatic.

To sound credible:

- Stay within the low to medium pitch.

- Go slower when substantiating a point, faster when making the point.

- Emphasise the key words where potential doubt may arise.

- Put in the right emotions to make a point. People believe the feeling more than the actual words you use.

To sound convincing:

- Start with high energy and enthusiasm. A slightly higher pitch at appropriate times will create this effect.

- Speed up at exciting points, or build up from a slow pace to create excitement.

- Put in powerful feelings and believe in what you are saying. The more you believe it yourself, the more others will be convinced.

- Pause before you make a strong closing statement, or before the call to action.

Speak powerfully

The sound of success is professional and also powerful. You will have realised by now that when we use the word power, it has nothing to do with dictatorial power. When you speak powerfully, you have control, and yet do not come across as controlling. When your boss says, "I want to see you at 9 am sharp tomorrow", he is controlling. If you have a report to rush, and would prefer to meet later, you could say, "I need to send a report to HQ first. Is it convenient for you if we meet at 9.30 am instead?" You are speaking powerfully without sounding controlling.

To sound powerful but not controlling, work on your language and consider how you phrase your words. Check this list of controlling words and phrases and see how they can be rephrased to sound more powerful:

Controlling	Powerful
You are wrong.	Let me explain why...
Why can't you see my point?	My reason is... what is yours?
I don't think this is a good idea.	Let's discuss some possible ideas.
We will meet today at 5 pm.	Are you available to meet at 5 pm today?
It won't work.	Let's consider other possible solutions.
You have to change your mind.	Let's consider the possible outcomes of your decision.
I demand an apology.	Let's discuss what caused you to make that comment, and see if we need to clarify our views.
I refuse to do it.	I recommend another way of doing it.

When you sound professional and powerful, people will be spontaneously drawn to you and will want to hire you, promote you or follow you. When you learn to use the right techniques and apply the lessons in this chapter, you are on your way to a polished professional image.

Star Tips for sounding professional

1. Evaluate the effectiveness of your current communication in projecting your brand values.

2. Enhance the technical and dramatic qualities of your voice.

3. Vary the pitch, volume, speed and range of your voice to create impact.

4. Start with your lowest pitch, and allow it to go higher when you need to.

5. Speak loudly enough for the person standing furthest away from you.

6. Vary your speed to create interest and build up excitement.

7. Use emphasis, emotions and pause to add dramatic effect on what you say.

8. Emphasise a key word with a change in pitch, volume or tone.

9. Connect with your listener by putting more feeling and emotion in a word.

10. Use pauses to grab attention, make a point, or invite a response.

YOUR PERSONALITY AND SUCCESS

"It's beauty that captures your attention; but personality that captures your heart."

Anonymous

Powerful brands are what they are today not just because of a nice sounding name and attractive packaging, but ultimately because they deliver what is promised. This is their intrinsic value, and brands that do not live up to customers' expectations will fall behind. When a brand connects with a consumer, it's as if it becomes human and has a personality that differentiates itself from competition.

In marketing research, consumers are often asked to personify their favourite brands, to help marketers understand what connects a brand to them. In focus group discussions, we ask consumers, "If this brand of car was an animal, what animal would it be?" We normally end up with one brand being associated with an elephant, which, in consumers' minds, is strong and sturdy, but rather slow and outdated. Another brand would be associated with a cheetah, which is seen to be sleek, fast and elegant.

That's how a brand's personality connects with a consumer to build brand loyalty. Just as a brand connects with a consumer through its personality, people in business connect in the same way. Our look may get us through the door, and our speech may help us in pitching our ideas, but we really seal the deal when our personality captures the heart. In this chapter, we will look at how your personality affects your behaviour at work and your connection with people.

Try This

Find out what people think of your personality by asking them to describe you as an animal. You can do this as a group exercise among your colleagues, and use it as a fun and insightful way to get feedback. Let them know you are open to hear their honest opinion and will not feel offended. Give each person a piece of paper and ask them to write down their thoughts on these questions (they need not give their names):

1. If I were an animal, what would it be?

2. What are the strengths of this animal that you feel I possess?

3. What are the weaknesses of this animal that I could overcome?

Now, collect the pieces of paper and read out each answer to the group. They may have a good laugh if there are some common responses, and you can ask for further feedback or clarification. If your colleagues are open to feedback like you are, you can use this exercise for teams who want to improve their teamwork and build a stronger bond.

What is your personality like?

There has been much research on the subject of personality, so I will not baffle you with another theory. There is also a diverse range of instruments available to measure personality type, some scientifically researched, and others just plucked from the air, or copied, or adapted. If you wish to know your personality type in detail, look for a reputable instrument, developed and tested by psychologists or specialists in this area. One such instrument is the Myers-Briggs Type Indicator (MBTI®), which I am qualified to administer, and is one of the most comprehensive and validated instruments I know. I strongly recommend you find the time to take the assessment, as it is extremely valuable in revealing your true self, helping you pinpoint what makes you act the way you do, and what makes people behave the way they do towards you.

Short of a personality assessment, how can we link personality to success? We do not carry a measuring tape around to work out people's personality type, and yet we seem to have no problem 'typing' people. We watch their behaviour. When we see someone cutting a queue (the behaviour), we describe the person as being inconsiderate and selfish. When someone becomes violent and abusive in an argument, he is seen as being aggressive. So, even if you do not know your personality type, you are being 'typed' every day, when people observe your behaviour.

To put it simply, your personality is reflected in your behaviour. According to Carl G Jung, the Swiss psychiatrist behind the original work of MBTI®, differences in our behaviour are a result of inborn tendencies to see the world and react to it in different ways. This explains why it's almost impossible to change a personality (husbands and wives know this as a fact). You can, however, change behaviour by changing the way you look at things.

Aha! Moment

Personality traits are inborn and they are the reason why we behave the way we do. When we understand our personality, we can change the way we see others, and adapt our behaviour accordingly.

Matching your personality to your brand values

People assess your personality through your behaviour. When your behaviour is consistent with your brand values, they will connect with your personality. When your behaviour is contrary to what you say you are, and not in sync with other people's expectations of you, they may not feel at ease in your company.

Let's review the Personality score in your VSP index, and look at your three brand values again. Read them out loud, and ask yourself these questions:

• Does my behaviour at work reflect these brand values?

• Do my relationships at work convey my brand values?

• How am I projecting my brand values in my business dealings?

If you need to work on your Personality index, examine your behaviour at work in the light of these questions, and consider how you can better reflect your brand values.

Let's take the example of an office manager whose brand values are Excellence, Empathy, and Honesty. He can assess how his behaviour is conveying these messages as shown here:

	Matching my brand values	**Not matching my brand values**
Behaviour at work	Punctual; organised; fast	Frequent typo errors
Relationships at work	Bonds well with my team	Mean to suppliers
Business dealings	Stick to company policies	Cover up mistakes

As you do this exercise, be as thorough as you can, and as honest as possible. For each of the categories above, you can drill down into specific behaviours. The more specific you are, the more it will reveal to you how your behaviour is affecting your success. Let's now look at each category of behaviour to see how you can let your personality shine.

Behaviour at work

Whether you are employed or work for yourself, your behaviour at work says a lot about who you are. Your behaviour may have nothing to do with your qualifications or experience. We assume that when you are hired or run your own business, you are good at what you do. Your employer, colleagues or customers have a minimum expectation of your performance. If there is a problem with your performance, you need to identify whether it has to do with your skills, or your behaviour.

I used to have a manager who could never send in his reports on time. He would always have an excuse, and no matter how urgent the client said it was, my manager would stretch the deadline for as long as he could. He would do things in his own time, and would merrily forget about deadlines if no one reminded him. I'm not surprised if there were reports he never submitted because the client had forgotten or left the company!

The problem he had was behavioural: he was actually good at writing. In fact, when his reports finally saw daylight, they were great! No amount of training could have helped if he did not see that his *poor* performance was due to his perception of time. To him, time was flexible, and whatever needed to be done could be done in his own time. Needless to say, he was transferred to another department where he worked alone, and had no clients to service or staff to supervise. It was certainly not the path of success for a manager.

Relationships at work

In my last role as Executive Director, before I started my own business, I was involved in developing both customer and employee satisfaction instruments for the company worldwide. We believed that successful companies achieved not just customer satisfaction, but also employee satisfaction. We used these instruments to help our clients figure out what factors had an impact on these two measurements. In almost all the surveys I was involved in, we found that the relationship factor was one of the key drivers affecting customer or employee satisfaction.

 Fast Fact

When an employee is happy in his job, he shows it in his attitude towards his work and makes the customer happy. When the customer is happy, he shows his appreciation and makes the employee happy. It's win-win all round!

In many cases, customers and employees said they leave or take their business elsewhere because of a relationship problem. As a customer, do you find that you sometimes put up with a less satisfying product because you have built a good relationship with the sales person? My mother is a good example: she has been to the same boutique for as long as I can remember, even though she could get better value clothes elsewhere.

Relationships at work are no different: people often leave their jobs due to dissatisfaction with their colleagues or boss. This is usually not the reason they give in exit interviews, but is often uncovered in anonymous surveys conducted by independent research companies. Is this true at your workplace? Do you find people whining more about their boss or colleagues, or about their salary? Do you know people who resign due to unhappiness with a boss or colleague, or due to the workload? If you probe further into the real reasons, they are probably linked to *how* people were treated, rather than *what* happened.

I'm not saying you don't need good quality products or a good salary to keep customers and employees happy. Or that you don't need to do a good job, only to be nice to people. What I'm saying is that despite the quality and value of your products, customers want to *feel good* when they buy from you or your company. And, despite your intelligence and competence, people want to *feel good* when they work with you.

While our personality has a lot to do with the way we relate to people, we cannot use this as an excuse for not getting along with someone. We need to find out what makes people tick, and learn to adapt to their preferences, to win them over. If you care about a relationship at work, you need to think of meeting others' needs first. When their needs are met, you have built a relationship, and your needs will eventually be met.

Business dealings

Whether you are a back-room or frontline staff, you are handling your company's business. Even if your work does not require you to interact with a customer, the way you handle your company's business reflects your level of professionalism. Your business dealings, whether internal or external, will affect people's perception of your character and personality. This in turn affects their decision to continue to work or do more business with you.

I used to work in a very competitive industry, and client confidentiality was a top priority in all our business dealings. It was so competitive that rival brands would prefer not to use the same research companies, to avoid a conflict of interest in the client servicing team. Survey respondents and even staff are screened to ensure they or their family members did not work for a competitor.

Keeping client confidentiality is essential in professional conduct, and should not be compromised in any form. This applies to you even if you are a buyer. If a company provides you with confidential information on their products and services, you must not give this to their competitor to get a lower price. I cringe when a potential customer says they want to send me a copy of a competitor's detailed proposal, as I hate to think that they would do the same with my proposal. My basic philosophy in business dealings boils down to two words: honesty and integrity.

Granted that what is considered acceptable business behaviour in one culture may be different from another, the universal guiding principle is to abide by the law of the country. If what you do is questionable under the law, you can safely say it is not professional business behaviour. Where there is ambiguity, always err on the side of the law.

 Danger Zone

When you do business in a culture that openly breaches confidentiality, or copyright laws, and it is seen to be socially acceptable, do not assume it is legal. Check the law or run the risk of a lawsuit on your hands.

Seven ways to behave professionally at work

No matter what your personality is like, there are certain behaviours at work that are expected of a professional. If these behaviours are not aligned with your personality, you may need to review your roadmap to reconsider the career path you are taking. If you are still determined to go down that path, then follow these seven steps to success:

1. **Be on time.** This shows respect for others. Even in a culture where time is more flexible, it's different in business. If you can catch a flight on time, you are capable of being punctual. You can wait for the plane, but the plane will not wait for you. If you are late for a job interview, you will never get the job. If you cannot meet a deadline, give sufficient notice so you don't keep others waiting.

2. **Deliver as promised.** You don't need to over- or under-promise; you just need to deliver as promised. If you can't do that, don't promise anything. It is better to turn down a request rather than face the consequences of not performing to expectations.

3. **Use company time for business only.** If you are an employee, your time during business hours belongs to the company. All personal e-mails, phone calls, errands or domestic affairs are best handled outside business hours. You are stealing from the company when you spend time on personal matters in the office.

4. **Spend the company's money with integrity.** Even if you have the authority to approve expenses, it doesn't mean you should make the most of it by spending every cent allocated in the budget. If you are given allowances to be reimbursed, you still need to show integrity by using it for designated purposes. Never claim personal entertainment under a business expense.

5. **Offer help when needed.** If a colleague or team member is incapacitated either through illness or unforeseen circumstances, chip in and offer to help. If it is within your capacity to do so, and if it does not jeopardise your own work, take it on without asking for compensation or a favour in return. If you are unable to help, find someone who can, or ask a senior officer for direction.

6. **Answer your colleague's phone.** When you know a colleague is not around or is busy with a task, don't let their phone ring non-stop. Pick it up! You never know who is on the line and how urgent it could be. Treat every phone call to the office as a business call and a potential business opportunity.

This could be an enquiry for a million dollar contract!

7. **Be responsive.** No matter what job you do, and whether you are a client or a supplier, your responsiveness will show how professional you are. Acknowledge an e-mail immediately, and if you can't give the response requested, suggest a date when you can do so. Return a phone call immediately, or inform the caller when you can talk. When you send a request and receive a response, show your appreciation with a note on your decision or action. In other words, let the other party know if they should keep waiting or move on without you.

Seven ways to build relationships at work

When you connect with people at work, you make it easier for them to want to work with you, or do business with you. When you understand your own personality, and how others may be different from you, you can adapt your behaviour to convey your brand values in the most powerful way. Here are seven powerful ways to build successful relationships at work:

1. **Listen first.** This is a really tough one, especially for extroverted personalities. Many a relationship is broken because no one listens, and each one thinks the other is at fault. When a customer is irate, or your colleague is not co-operative, stop and listen to what they are saying. They could be wrong, but so could you.

2. **Be considerate.** To connect with someone, think of them first, then yourself. Even when you are the buyer, be considerate to the seller. Nobody owes you a living, but they will bend the rules and go the extra mile for you when you show consideration. Talking too loudly, cracking off-colour jokes, leaving a mess, humiliating people in public, smoking in a non-smoking area, parking in a no-parking zone, asking for a report on Friday afternoon to be sent to you by Monday morning: these are just some examples of inconsiderate behaviour.

3. **Connect with your eyes.** It is said that the eyes are the windows to your soul. While some cultures may consider direct eye contact as being domineering, in business it can be very powerful for making the right connections. Used in the right context, the eyes can send positive messages to create rapport and build trust in a relationship. If you don't believe me, try saying, "I love you" to your beloved without looking at them in the eye.

Try This

To send the right message and say what you really mean, practise with a friend and say the following pairs of words by using eye contact. Note how the eyes change with each change of word:

Happy, Sad

Love, Hate

Peace, War

Generous, Selfish

Abundance, Poverty

4. **Adopt a really good attitude.** It is amazing how attitude drives behaviour. Attitude is the first thing people notice in communication. It may seem intangible, and you can't quite measure it, but you know when someone relates to you, whether they have a good or bad attitude. Parents know what it feels like when a child answers back — the behaviour shows an attitude of disrespect. It is usually not what is said that hurts, but the attitude behind it. Attitude is also infectious, so when you show a really great attitude every time you meet someone, they cannot help but give you the same in return.

5. **Use open body language.** These are the silent messages you send that work wonders to create a positive rapport. Some examples of open body language are standing up to greet people, facing palms up and open, removing obstacles that are blocking your view of each other, and nodding. Open body language says you have nothing to hide, you are approachable, and ready to build a positive relationship.

6. **Find common ground.** When you meet someone for the first time, it is natural to look for common ground so you can start a conversation. The minute both of you discover you were educated in the same school, or born in the same month, or have a mutual friend, you start to connect. With a customer, you can also look for common ground to build a good relationship — you never know how loyal they can be when you establish a connection. Many employees have followed their bosses as they get transferred, or join another company, all because they have found common ground on which to stay connected.

7. **Get them talking.** Again, a very tough one for extroverted people. I am an extrovert, but when I meet another extrovert, I know I have to shut up, or lose them in the conversation. If you talk all the time, and don't give others a chance, you risk losing their attention and interest in what you are saying. To keep your sanity, listen while they are talking, and ask questions to connect with them. By asking questions intermittently, you show interest in them, and make them feel important. It is also a great way to find out more about their personality and their needs, and to build a stronger relationship.

Seven ways to show professionalism in business dealings

1. **Be honest.** Only you know what is the truth, and how much you need to reveal to achieve your objectives. Only you know if your actions and behaviour are intentionally deceitful for personal gains. People will not do business with someone they suspect has misled them.

2. **Be accountable.** Take responsibility for any task entrusted to you. Unless you have been forced to take on a job, you are accountable for the outcome. If you have delegated it to someone else, it is still your responsibility if the job is not done. If you are the leader, you

need to be on top of what's going on, and be prepared to take action when things are not moving. You connect with people when they know they can count on you.

3. **Offer solutions to problems.**   When problems arise, be the first to ask, "How can we resolve this?" and the last to find blame. Treat all problems as opportunities for both you and the company to show how good you really are. Your approach to problem-solving differentiates you from competition. Once resolved, a relationship can only get stronger, and people will be indebted to you.

4. **Give extra value.**   When in a negotiation, offer a little extra value, instead of taking away something. This need not cost you or your company any extra money, and is within your empowerment to do. Be creative and look for ways to do something extra — it goes a long way to building relationships.

5. **Show you care.**   No matter what industry you are in, what products you sell, we are all in the people business. Be they your boss, employees, colleagues or customers, they need to know you care for them in all your dealings. Every organisation must make provision for showing care and concern for their employees and customers. This is the soft touch that cannot be replaced by a machine or electronic gadget. Even the online business needs to connect with people in a real way.

6. **Compete fairly.** Unless you are in a monopoly, treat all competition with respect. Do not spy on your competition, or get information unethically. Worse still, do not copy or steal information from competitors. People who buy from copycats do not appreciate the real value of your

product, and therefore will not make loyal customers, as they will jump ship the minute they find a cheaper copycat. Build relationships on the authenticity of your offer.

 Myth Buster

Everyone is buying pirated products, so it must be acceptable.

Well, many wrongs don't make it right. Whether you make or buy pirated products, you are diminishing the value of the original work. If you are professional, you need to uphold and support the work of professionals and not copycats.

7. **Embrace diversity.** This is the buzz in the 21st century for organisations to embrace differences in culture, ways of life, preferences, and social status. It calls for fair treatment regardless of gender, age, skin colour, or other demographics. While it is idealistic, multi-national companies around the world have put policies in place to hire based on merit, and not demographics. You too can do your part, even if your organisation or the country you live in has not moved in this direction. When you treat everyone as unique, regardless of where they come from, you capture the heart.

If you have been following each chapter up to this point, you would have developed a pretty good package by now. Your package will be looking professional, sounding professional and behaving like a professional. This is what we call a personal brand. If you are satisfied with the image you have developed so far, it's time to move on to look at how you can position your brand for success.

Star Tips for behaving professionally

1. Review your brand values to examine if they are reflected in your work behaviour, relationships and business dealings.

2. Identify the behaviours that do not match your brand values, and work to improve the level of professionalism.

3. Show professional behaviour by being on time, delivering as promised, and being responsive.

4. Identify your relationship with colleagues and customers, and work on those that do not match your brand values.

5. Be professional in developing work relationships by listening, being considerate and putting on a good attitude.

6. Build positive rapport with eye contact, open body language and finding common ground.

7. Identify the behaviours in your business dealings that do not match your brand values, and work towards a professional standard.

8. Treat all client information as confidential.

9. Be professional in your business dealings by showing honesty, being accountable, offering solutions and competing fairly.

10. Treat people professionally by showing care, giving extra value, and embracing diversity.

POSITIONING YOUR BRAND FOR SUCCESS

"The easiest thing in the world to be is you. The most difficult thing to be is what other people want you to be. Don't let them put you in that position."

Leo F. Buscaglia

I recently attended a reunion dinner with former mates of the university hostel where I spent four years of my young adult life. After more than 30 years, you can imagine how unrecognisable some people were. Most had put on a few inches and pounds (including me), but some looked almost like they did 30 years ago! What hardly changed, though, were their personalities — we may have forgotten some names, but their mannerisms and behaviour immediately jogged our memory as to who they were.

When recalling a person, we mentally search for cues to associate with him or her. As we discussed in Chapter 1, somewhere in the brain we store a 'box' of all the images of this person. The minute we recall this box, we form certain expectations of what he should look like or be like. If it doesn't match our memory, we say, "You have changed a lot!" If it does, we gladly declare, "You are still the same as before!"

The expectation of what we should be is how people place us in their box — in marketing, this is known as positioning. When people form an impression of us, they also have some expectations. If we can manage these perceptions, we can achieve the success we want and be who we want to be. Let's now look at how we can review our personal brand and position it for success.

Dare to be different

Every consumer brand has a positioning in the market, and this is defined as the identity it has created in the minds of its consumers. When we think of a brand like Prada, we immediately associate it with distinction, luxury and high-class. When we think of Singapore Airlines, we think of service, global reach, and leading-edge aviation technology. World-class companies spend millions of dollars on their brand positioning so they can carve an identity that differentiates them from the competition.

Does this mean you have to do something similar with your personal brand? Well, not to the same extent, but it certainly needs strategic planning and effort to create a strong positioning. This is the difference between having an image and having a brand positioning. As discussed in the beginning of this book, we all have an image. If we don't do anything about this image, people will form whatever impressions or expectations they have and place this in their mental box. However, if we create an identity that differentiates ourselves in terms of our professional image, then we have a brand positioning.

Positioning is a way of telling your specific target market what you stand for and what is your brand promise. When people know your brand positioning, they can decide if they want to work with you or conduct business with you. What we say about ourselves is what we call the brand positioning statement. Now, let's look at how you can develop a strong positioning statement for your personal brand.

The 4 W's in your brand positioning statement

You have probably written a brand positioning statement before without realising it. When you write a resumé, it is a form of brand positioning. When you introduce yourself, you are making a brand positioning statement. When you start your own business, your website or marketing collaterals describe your brand positioning. If you have any of these, look through them to see if they are crafted to project your brand values. Ask yourself how you can you revise them to project a stronger brand positioning. When developing your brand positioning statement, you need to include the 4 W's:

1. What is your brand promise?

This is a description of what you can offer, not just what you do. If you want your application letter or resumé to stand out from the crowd, you must let your potential employer know what makes you different. When you introduce yourself, you will create more interest if you say what you can offer, rather than just what you do. What's special about you? What unique strengths do you bring to the company or potential employer? What are the benefits of hiring you or buying from you?

2. Why should they believe you?

It is easy to say what you can offer, so you need to substantiate it with evidence. This typically comprises your credentials, i.e. your qualifications, experience, and skills. Select the relevant information to support your brand promise. At an interview, you need to show how your credentials will enable you to deliver your brand promise. Be relevant, and mention only those credentials or achievements that matter to your audience. Nobody wants to see a long list that has no meaning or relevance to the situation.

3. Who are you targeting?

The most disappointing application letters for recruiters are those written to no one. You can spot them easily as they say nothing about how the job-seeker would fit into the potential employer's organisation. You know it is the same letter sent to every recruiter, addressed *'to whom it may concern'*. Sometimes, they even forget to change the job title or the company to whom they are applying. To stand out and be noticed, you need to revise each application letter or resumé to address a specific target audience. Similarly, when introducing yourself to a group, you want to address how you fit in, by relating what you do to their organisation.

4. Where can you contribute most?

A very powerful way to differentiate yourself is to let people know where you can make the most contribution. No one should claim that they can work in any organisation, any sector, any location, and be everything to everyone. Nobody wants to hire you when you say you can do any job, at any location, at any salary. Sure, some people may have a breadth of experience and exposure to say that. If you don't have this, then name specific areas of experience or expertise that will appeal to your target audience. This can be an industry or sector, a specialised area, a physical location, or even an environment.

Fast Fact

Recruiters spend less than 10 seconds deciding whether a resumé deserves their attention. If it does not show why they should hire you in less than 10 seconds, it goes into the bin. Give your resumé an image makeover by enhancing the 4 W's.

Positioning your resumé for success

As a department head, I used to be involved in screening job applications. For each job vacancy, the human resource department screens out those who don't meet the minimum criteria (e.g. if a bachelor's degree is a pre-requisite, and the applicant only has 'A' level certification). After the pre-screening, I would still have to screen a few hundred applications to shortlist three to five people for an interview. I had a simple system called the 'knock-out system'. This involved dividing the applications into two piles: 'knock-out' and 'finalist' piles. The easiest part of this task was deciding which application went to the knock-out pile. If I found a typo error on my company's name, it went straight to the knock-out pile. If the date was wrong, you know where it went. If the document looked cluttered and was too long, it was 'knocked out'.

It would take me only a few seconds per application to decide which pile it went. I didn't read the applications in the knock-out pile at all. This system would usually result in about eight to 10 applicants in the finalist pile, which I would take the time to read, and then make a final shortlist. These applicants were selected because they were able to position their resumés for success.

Now, examine your resumé using the 4 W's. If you were the recruiter, would you be impressed? Do all the 4 W's address the needs of the potential employer? What would make the reader want to put you in their finalist pile? Is your resumé a standard template you use for every job application? Does it reflect your brand values?

Here are five tips to add a touch of professionalism to your resumé, and position your brand for success:

1. **Summarise your brand promise at the beginning.** This is sometimes referred to as the *objective statement*. This should grab attention. Keep it short, to the point, and state what you offer. Adapt this according to the potential employer so they can see the benefits of hiring you.

2. **Present your credentials.** Highlight any details that are relevant to the specific job you are applying for. List your major achievements, and only mention details where relevant, e.g. a subject you majored in or a project you handled. Grades are not necessary unless requested.

3. **Mention direct implications for the job you are applying for.** When listing achievements, mention those that have implications for the job you are applying for. This is where you can demonstrate your potential contribution to the company. Be specific and factual so as not to sound boastful. Be careful not to give away confidential information, and keep it short and relevant.

4. **Send a short covering letter with your resumé.** Always customise your letter to address the employer. Mention briefly your brand promise and why they should choose you.

5. **Spellcheck and proofread for accuracy.** Before you send, take care to check carefully to make sure there are no errors. Your resumé goes straight to the bin if it has spelling, grammatical or typographical mistakes. Check your formatting to make it easy for the reader to read and find information. It must look professional if it is to stand out!

Myth Buster

A resumé is just a factual document of my background and credentials. Recruiters want all the details so they can compare each applicant on their qualifications and experience. The more details I provide, the better my resumé will be.

You've missed the opportunity if you think this way! To stand out from the crowd, your resumé must show you are the person for the job. Make it look like you customise it for your potential employer, not just any employer.

So far, we've examined the brand positioning for job seekers. The same process can be applied to any other form of brand positioning. After you've got the job, you need to continually update your brand positioning, for the next promotion or next career. To do that, it will be good to have ready a brand positioning statement. This is sometimes referred to as an 'elevator statement'.

Positioning your elevator statement for success

The term 'elevator statement' originated from the idea of having a short span of time (i.e. the duration of an elevator ride) to introduce yourself or your company to a potential employer or buyer. An elevator statement is intended to create the greatest impact to a specific audience, in the shortest amount of time. It is useful to have an elevator statement, prepared and rehearsed, for unexpected opportunities where you may have to introduce yourself or your company.

Using the 4 W's, you can write your elevator statement to position yourself for success.

What is your brand promise? ➡

Why should they believe you? ➡

Who are you targeting? ➡

Where can you contribute? ➡

My name is _____. I am _____.

I offer/provide/make/enable_____.

I have_____years' experience in_____.

and am qualified/specialised in_____ .

My passion/vision is _____.

I have worked with_____ (industry/customers/trade) and in_____ (country/region).

Once you have a standard elevator statement, you can adapt it to any situation. In some cases, it may be impromptu, when you are asked to give a short introduction of yourself and what you do. Try to avoid saying, "My name is _____ and I am just a _____. That's all." Instead use your standard elevator statement. Imagine how you would stand out from the crowd, especially when you give your brand promise!

In other situations, you may be notified in advance, or you may be meeting a new contact who is important to your future career. You can then review your standard elevator statement to adapt it according to *who* you are meeting. This can also be used as an introduction before you make a presentation. It's a great opportunity to position your brand and differentiate yourself from other presenters.

Keep in mind that an elevator statement is designed to be short, so use it only when the time given to you is restricted. For greatest effectiveness, keep it within 60 seconds, and have a 30 seconds version ready if there is a roomful of people introducing themselves.

Try This

Rehearse your elevator statement in front of a mirror. If necessary, put on the appropriate clothes to project your brand positioning. Work on your voice to project the professional image you want. Check your body language, put on a really good attitude, and practice your elevator speech till you sound like a polished professional.

Positioning your bio for success

A bio is another great opportunity to position your brand. This could be used on a company website, brochure, or a proposal. It can also be used if someone else were to introduce you either as a presenter or in an official capacity. Early in my career when I was a speaker at a seminar, I had sent my bio to the organiser in advance to give my introduction. When I arrived, I learnt that the person who prepared the introduction was going to be late, and someone else had taken his place. I thought all was well until he stood up, stammered from beginning to end, not knowing what to say about me. He lacked confidence and spoke in broken English, giving a very unprofessional start to my talk. I decided from that day onwards, I would never let someone introduce me if they could not present a professional image of me!

Danger Zone

Don't allow someone else to introduce you at an important event if they did not prepare a script and rehearse it with you. If you feel the person is not fit to give the introduction, it is better to do it yourself than risk being sabotaged by a poor introduction.

Never let this happen to you. Always ask who is introducing you, and give them your script. If possible, run through the introduction with them before you come on. If the situation calls for it, and you are not satisfied with the introducer, take over and do it yourself.

So how can your present yourself professionally in your bio? Use the 4 W's to write your bio in your style. If somebody writes it for you, it will not come out naturally when you speak. If you need professional help, write it first and then ask someone to vet it. Here are five tips on positioning your bio for success:

1. **Start with who you are — your position or role in the company.** This helps the audience to place you and know where you are coming from. For example:

   Paul Tan is Marketing Manager for ABC Manufacturing, and is responsible for the overall marketing and advertising divisions.

2. **Follow soon after with your brand promise.** This can be incorporated in a paragraph on your experience or your credentials, depending on its relevance. It is more interesting to make a statement of what you can offer, backed by a real experience or qualification. For example:

   Paul drives the division with his creative leadership and global vision, having managed the company's expansion into the Asia Pacific region. In this capacity as team leader in this project, he has contributed to a 20 per cent growth in the past year.

3. **Mention relevant credentials in the context of the purpose of the bio.** If it is for a general publicity material, highlight the key qualifications

and experience. If it is for a seminar, highlight the credentials relevant to the topic of your speech. If it is for a proposal, give more details to substantiate your brand promise. For example:

> Paul comes with eight years of experience in the marketing and advertising field. Prior to joining ABC, he spent five years with an international advertising agency, responsible for several major client accounts. Paul's creative flair is evident in the many advertising awards won by his clients.

4. **Customise each bio according to the target audience.** This means that you need to adapt a standard bio for different purposes. If it is for a sales pitch, you need to mention how your contribution will make a difference to the company, and what specific needs you can meet. If it is for a presentation, you must mention how you can address the audience's needs. For example:

> Paul is a dynamic and inspirational team leader, having led numerous project teams locally and regionally. We are confident Paul will bring energy and insights to this seminar.

5. **Unless it is crucial to the audience, or purpose, academic qualifications need not be mentioned up front.** For a general target audience, or where it is important to establish your credibility, it is best to leave it at the end of the bio. For example:

> Paul holds a Bachelor of Marketing from the University of Singapore.

Try This

If you have never written a bio before, start writing one now, using the steps and examples given. If you already have one, review it to see if you have addressed the following:

1. What is the purpose of this bio? Use your credentials to support the purpose.

2. Who is the intended target audience? Use an approach to interest the audience you are addressing.

3. What credentials and experience would the audience like to know?

Positioning your brand for a promotion

I used to work for a multi-national company with 100 offices around the globe. In my 11 years of working there, we had seen mergers, acquisitions and re-mergers. It was originally a management-owned company, and in those days it was easy to figure out who would be next in line for promotion. If you were good, you would soon be rewarded with a promotion. However, as soon as new management took over, the old guards found themselves replaced by young and aspiring high-flyers from overseas.

Sadly, many did not know how to position or re-position themselves to the new management, so they lost their jobs, or were overlooked in the new line-up. Perhaps, in Asia, it is also culturally embarrassing to openly ask for a promotion, as people fear they may *lose face* if the request is turned down. So how do you compete in an environment where some of your colleagues are more aggressive in rising to the top than you are? How can you let your employer know you are ready for that promotion without overtly saying so?

Here are five steps on how to nab that promotion:

1. Review your brand promise, and write a future brand positioning statement. Re-phrase it according to the future position you wish to be promoted to.

2. Determine what credentials you need (either experience or further qualifications) to be able to substantiate your future brand promise.

3. Offer to take on tasks or responsibilities to give you the experience you need, or go for further training to acquire new skills required for the new position.

4. Find out what your future boss is looking for in the position you want. Keep track of your performance in step 3, and ask for feedback on how you are doing in the new areas.

5. Start making changes to your professional image so that you look, sound and behave like your future position. When the management can see your transformation to fit into that role, you will be the obvious choice, without having to ask for it.

 Aha! Moment

If I feel I deserve a promotion, I can work on my brand positioning to show my future boss that I am ready for a new position.

In this chapter, we have focussed on developing a strong positioning for your brand that will make you stand out from the rest of the pack. Now that you have a great positioning statement, it's time to get it out there and let people know you exist, and why you are so great. If you wait for the next job advertisement before writing your resumé, or your bio, you are only being reactive. In the next chapter, we will look at how you can be proactive and learn the art of self-promotion.

Star Tips for positioning your brand for success

1. Differentiate yourself by developing a strong brand positioning statement.

2. State what your brand promise is, and what you can offer.

3. Give reasons why people should hire you or buy from you.

4. Address your brand positioning statement to a specific audience.

5. Indicate where you can contribute the most — be specific.

6. Customise your resume to show your potential employer why they should hire you.

7. Prepare and rehearse your elevator statement for unexpected opportunities to position your brand for success.

8. Prepare your bio to represent your brand values and professional image.

9. Make a statement of what you offer, and back it up with your credentials.

10. Develop a future brand positioning statement to position yourself for a promotion.

THE ART OF
SELF-PROMOTION

"To establish oneself in the world, one does all one can to seem established there already."

François de La Rochefoucauld

I had my share of missed opportunities in my younger days, simply because I didn't know how to make myself known without sounding boastful. The most unforgettable one was when I earned myself a spot in one of the top schools in Singapore for my 'A' levels, or what was then known as pre-university. The school was (and still is) a well-known boys' school at the secondary level, and they only began accepting girls into its 'A' levels the year before I joined. I had come from a girls' school and, as you can imagine, was overwhelmed not just by the fact that I was in a premier school, but also one where girls were in the minority.

As I was learning to get used to the idea of being quite a nobody in the school, and going about the daily routine, a school prefect appeared in my classroom one morning, and summoned me to meet the prefectorial board! My heart pounding, and thinking the worst, I reluctantly dragged my feet to the daunting meeting, wondering what I had done wrong. My fears soon subsided when the head prefect welcomed me warmly, and informed me that I had been nominated to be a prefect. However, I was one out of four female nominees, and they would hold an election in two weeks, among the girls only, to select just two.

Instead of being elated and excited about this opportunity, I spent the next two weeks wondering who nominated me and why. How did they know me when I came from an unknown girls' school? Why me when there were so many girls, many smarter and more outstanding than me? Why would the other girls elect me when I was an unknown? When election day came, I had not prepared my speech. I wasn't used to campaigning, and felt it was too arrogant to tell people how good I was and why I was better than the other nominees. I can't remember a word I said. Needless to say, I didn't get elected.

Aha! Moment

Self-promotion is not about bragging, or deceiving others to think you are better than what you really are. It is also not about bad-mouthing your competition, but about establishing what your unique strengths are, compared to competition.

That was my first big lesson on the art of self-promotion. To this day, I remember this lesson more than anything else I learnt during those two years in pre-university! That is, to succeed, you have to behave like you have succeeded. You have to think like a winner, not a loser. If you don't tell others how good you are, or can be, how would they know? If you don't ask them to choose you, why should they?

In this chapter, we will focus on the proactive part of personal branding, and show you how to master the art of self-promotion. You will identify the appropriate channels to promote yourself, and take steps to project yourself professionally to each target audience.

Channels for self-promotion

If you have faced a similar situation in your career where an opportunity arose, and you missed it because you were not prepared to promote yourself, it's because you were *reactive*. If you don't want to miss another golden opportunity, it's time to start working on a *proactive* plan to promote yourself. Let's start with the various forms of creating a presence in the marketplace:

Physical presence

Print presence

Media presence

Virtual presence

Physical presence

Despite the advent of technology and e-business, which enables offices to operate without being in physical touch with employees or customers, nothing beats interacting with people. The old saying, "Out of sight, out of mind" still holds true in today's competitive environment. Just like consumer products that need to have a high visibility to stay top-of-mind in consumers' heads, you too need to create a strong physical presence to be noticed and remembered. For potential employers or customers to keep you top-of-mind when an opportunity arises, you need to be out there, and be seen.

I am not referring to just showing up at the office every day, because that is expected of you. I am talking about proactively meeting people even outside of the office, networking within and outside the company, being active in the industry or community, and getting connected with people at a personal and professional level.

Fast Fact

Researchers have found that positive human contact reduces the blood levels of the stress hormones. When we feel the connection with somebody in person, it increases the level of hormones that create trust and bonding.

Print presence

While you can only be in one place at a time, your print presence works for you even when you are asleep, on holiday, or too busy to meet up. People may forget your face, name or what you do, but if you have it in print as well, they can be reminded of your presence. Notwithstanding the power of telecommunications, anything in print is more tangible and has a captive audience when presented attractively and effectively. To create a strong print presence, find the channel that works for you in your particular area or industry. These can range from simple forms like a business card, flyers and brochures, to more sustainable and powerful channels like publishing a book.

Media presence

The media can be a very influential channel for promoting your professional image. With its various forms, from print to broadcasting, you can create an impressive presence with the right messages. You can select from a diverse range of media channels to reach the right target audience, and develop messages that appeal to them. If you are already a known personality in your field, the media will contact you for news or features. If not, you could send press releases to get their attention, or send articles or information to the appropriate media for publicity.

Virtual presence

It is mind-boggling how business can take place across the globe without anyone stepping out of his or her office (or home). If you work remotely, or your work does not require you to have face-to-face interactions, then you will probably have to rely heavily on your virtual presence to help you project a powerful professional image. If people don't get to meet you, you want to make sure they remember you and are accessible to them when they need you. This means projecting a positive image consistently through all electronic channels, including e-mails, telephone, video-conferencing, and social media like blogs and twitter. This can also be a very powerful medium for those who have less opportunity to meet people, and if used effectively, it can create a world-wide audience for you without even having to step out of the door.

Creating a strong professional presence

Let's now look at how you can be proactive in creating a strong professional presence, using any of these channels. There are three broad audiences you can reach out to:

Reach out to people within your organisation

By this I mean any human contact that is taking place within your organisation, including contact with colleagues, customers and suppliers. This includes local or overseas, and within or outside the physical office. Apart from the day-to-day contacts that are necessary for business, you can create many opportunities to make contact with people. It means making an effort to connect with people, or taking the initiative to establish a relationship, even if there is no formal business or work to discuss. Here are some simple and proactive ideas you can start to implement.

- **Lunch with different colleagues.** Most of us are guilty of lunching with the same people every day, or worse still, with no one at all. I observed this pattern in all the organisations where I've worked. It is only natural to find the same lunch partners, because you know you won't be rejected. On the other hand, if you were a newcomer, it would be difficult to join an existing group that is not inclusive. You can be proactive by having lunch with different colleagues, and making an effort to get to know people on a personal level. Is there anyone in your organisation who might feel excluded? Give him or her a call today, and ask if he or she would like to join your group for lunch.

 Danger Zone

If you are inviting a member of the opposite sex for lunch for the first time, be careful not to send the wrong signals. If possible, lunch with a group, or go to a casual place. Even if you have a special interest in someone, make your moves outside the office, and do not become exclusive during lunchtime.

- **Introduce yourself to people you've not met before.** If you work in a big organisation, you will probably not get to meet every single colleague. You may ride in the same elevator, take the same train to work, or even live in the same neighbourhood, but never speak to each other because you work in different departments. However, you'd be surprised how nice most people are when you offer a handshake, smile and introduce yourself, by saying, "Hi, we've not met before. My name is _____", and give your elevator statement. Now, start making a list of people in your organisation you've not met before, and find a way to bump into them.

 Try This

Go through your company directory and check how many people you have met. Do a little survey and indicate:

1. How many people do you know and have met?

2. How many people do you know of, but have never met?

3. How many people would you not recognise if you saw them outside the office (e.g. you were introduced before but you cannot remember their face)?

Now, make a list of people you would like to meet, and find an opportunity to get to know them.

- **Get involved in company activities or events.** All organisations create opportunities for colleagues to interact outside business, and your participation will be highly appreciated when you show you are a sport instead of a 'party-pooper'. Even if you are introverted and reserved, you can still get involved by volunteering for a role you are comfortable with. I used to have a boss who never liked socialising, but he would still be a sport and show up for all our social events. He would decline to dance (even if we physically dragged him onto the dance floor), and would just sit by himself enjoying his beer, and watch the rest of us have a good time. His presence alone was enough to say he cared about being with us, even though he was not comfortable with our activities. So, mark on your calendar what company activities you will volunteer to get involved in during the coming year.

- **Connect with other stakeholders.** Everyone you have a business relationship with in your organisation provides an opportunity for you to promote yourself. In all situations, stay within the code of business and professional ethics, and keep every activity above board. If budget allows, and it is within your capacity, meet your customers or suppliers for lunch, or for a drink after work. In some organisations, it's not ethical to entertain a potential client, so you could suggest 'going dutch' (each person pays for their own meal). I have developed some strong friendships through connecting with external stakeholders in this way, and some of my former clients are still good friends up to this day. So, go through your mailing list and make a point to connect with the important stakeholders in your organisation.

Reach out to people within your industry

Once you've got into the habit of connecting with people within your organisation, you can start thinking about making your presence known within your industry. This is the best place to start if you are not used to promoting yourself, because you should be most comfortable with people in your own field. It is easier to start a conversation with someone in the same occupation or industry. Here are some proactive and effective ways to establish a presence in your industry:

- **Join an association.**   Birds of a feather do flock together, so in any location where you work, there must be a gathering of like-minded people you could join. It may be an official or unofficial group, as long as you share some common interests related to your work or career. If you are a secretary or an administrative professional, there must be an association of secretaries who would warmly welcome you as a member. If you are an accountant working in the advertising industry, you could join an accounting association or an advertising association. If you are not comfortable with face-to-face interactions, you can join online groups or forums related to your industry. Be proactive and search the Internet for groups or associations in your industry that you could potentially join and establish new relationships.

- **Get involved in industry events.**   There are plenty of these around, and you need to be selective so that you spend your time wisely with the right target audience. Conferences, seminars and trade shows are typical examples of industry events. Give top priority to events your organisation is involved in, and volunteer to speak, man a booth, or even be an usher. Ask your company to sponsor you for events that could benefit your company. If you run your own business, you may want to consider investing in a key event that could help you establish a strong presence. Keep your eyes open for top-notch industry events, either locally or overseas, and set aside some budget in your business plan to attend the next one.

- **Contribute to the industry.**   This can be in many forms, and need not be monetary. You could contribute your time by volunteering for a committee role, taking up leadership, or writing articles for an industry newsletter. You could also tap on media opportunities to be a contact or spokesperson for your industry group, or contribute articles to industry magazines. This is a very effective way to demonstrate your strengths and expertise, and at the same time establish your presence in the industry. Consider your options and decide what specific contribution you can make to help grow your industry.

- **Create strategic alliances.**   Some industries are highly competitive, and this makes it difficult for competitors to meet socially and pretend they are not fighting for the same rice bowl. I used to be in one such industry where we could not mingle with anyone from a competitor company without being suspected of treason. In such cases, you can create opportunities for a strategic alliance with competitors to achieve a win-win relationship. Some examples of strategic alliances are a joint conference or seminar, forums, customer groups, or a joint research project. Contact people in the industry and suggest a meeting to brainstorm ideas for a strategic alliance.

Myth Buster

If I get involved in an industry project with a competitor, my company will accuse me of having a conflict of interest.

This is very conservative thinking and can exist only in a monopoly. To avoid any misperception of your intentions, check with your boss on the guidelines for business conduct, and keep your interactions above board.

Reach out to the wider community

At this stage, I need you to step out of your comfort zone, and step into the big wide world. The opportunities to promote yourself are in abundance if you only look hard enough. Perhaps this is what William Shakespeare meant when he penned the words, "Why then, the world's my oyster, which I with sword will open." You may have your own interpretation of this, but my take from it is that the opportunities are out there in the world, outside your comfort zone, and to find your 'oyster', you need to open it (with the sword). The 'oyster' could be your dream career, your aspiration, or your wealth. The 'sword' represents a proactive step in using the right tool to open up the 'oyster'. You too, can open your world of oysters when you learn to approach the world outside your industry with the right professional image. Here are some proactive ideas to help you expand your world of influence:

- **Join networking groups.**   There are hundreds of networking groups for a broad spectrum of industries or interests. This gives you exposure to people outside your own field, and creates opportunities for you to establish your presence without fear of rivalry. Most networking groups have specific objectives, and you should find one that is compatible with your own objectives. Some examples of such groups are Business Networking International (BNI), speed networking groups, Chamber of Commerce business groups, private clubs, and many others. Again, if you don't enjoy meetings, you can join online networking groups like LinkedIn and Plaxo. Search the Internet for networking groups you can join to expand your horizons.

- **Get involved in other industry events.**   Like your own industry, these opportunities can be enormous, and sometimes overwhelming. So choose wisely which industry you can establish a strong presence in. It could be a related industry (e.g. advertising and public relations), or it could be an industry you have an interest in, or where your potential customers may come from. The possibilities are limited only by your imagination and capability. Identify where you can best contribute (e.g. public speaking, writing articles, or administrative work), and offer your expertise in your targeted industry. Review your career goals and identify any potential industry you can join or get involved in, and establish a new presence.

- **Get involved in the community.** These can range from charity groups to purely social groups. You could join a neighbourhood watchdog team, or volunteer in a local charity organisation, or simply just take part in a community festival. The key point is to know people and to get yourself known in the community at large. Again, if you are not into social activities, you can always offer to do something in your comfort zone (e.g. taking attendance or arranging logistics). Your presence will still be felt without you having to do too much. Consider carefully your personal interest and genuine desire to give to the community, and involve yourself in areas where you feel you can contribute most.

It's not about you

In case you are now all gung-ho to sign up with every association or networking event in town to let the whole world know all about you, I want to consider just one more caveat. You will only be successful in achieving your professional goals if your underlying purpose is to serve others, not your personal ambitions. While I urge you to be proactive in promoting yourself, my utmost desire is for you to think of others first. This is the mark of true professionalism. This will differentiate you from a self-important bragger, who is so full of himself, and bulldozes his way to get all the attention, with no consideration for anyone else. While you start taking action in your personal branding, do note the following guidelines to reflect your professional image:

1. **Add a personal touch in all your contacts**. Whether you are using the e-mail, phone, a blog, or physical meeting, put the audience first. In today's electronic age, things are happening so fast that we may forget there is a human at the receiving end. Take care to craft your message, even your elevator statement, with the audience in mind.

2. **Use the appropriate channel according to the impact desired.** If you are inviting a new colleague to lunch, a personal visit to her office or desk is much better than an e-mail.

3. **Always have your business cards with you.** Never leave the office without them. It's considered rude not to give your card at a business meeting or event.

4. **Mind your manners, whether physically or electronically.** Everything we discussed in Chapter 7 applies here. Even if you are at a social event, and think that you can misbehave because you're not at work, think again. Someone there could be a potential customer or employer who would immediately write you off with unprofessional behaviour.

5. **Be prepared at all times with your elevator statement.** If you are caught tongue-tied when asked what you do, you have missed an opportunity. Think about the audience you are about to meet, and mentally list a few things you want to say or talk about so that you interest them.

6. **Check every communication you send out, whether in print or electronic form, to make sure it represents your brand values and image.** A potential client or employer may have access to your blog, facebook, or other media, and will get mixed messages if they are not consistent with the image you project at work.

7. **Ensure consistency in your professional look.** This applies whether you are attending a business meeting or social event. Even when dressing casually, you still need to project the same brand values. You never know which potential customer or employer you might meet at a family day, or a Christmas party.

8. **Ensure consistency in the way you sound.** If you speak differently at work and at lunch, people will suspect you are faking one or the other. A good example is someone who speaks with a very strong, unnatural accent when making a presentation.

If you have been diligent so far in developing your professional image and taking action to promote your personal brand, you have reached a major milestone in your life. Congratulations! You are on your way to reaching the vision and goals you set at the beginning of this book. However, if you are struggling with some steps, it could be because you are facing some roadblocks in your life at this point. Let's move on to the final chapter where I will help you to remove these roadblocks and clear the path to success.

Star Tips for promoting your personal brand

1. Be proactive in developing a plan to promote your personal brand inside and outside your organisation.

2. Create a strong physical presence within your organisation by establishing contact with people outside your immediate work area.

3. Create a strong physical presence within your industry by getting involved in associations or industry events.

4. Create a strong physical presence in the wider community by getting involved in charity organisations, other industry or community events.

5. Reach out to a wider audience by enhancing your print presence.

6. Establish a strong presence among the public by using the appropriate media channel.

7. Expand your virtual presence by tapping on the power of e-communication tools.

8. Keep in mind your audience's interest first in all your contacts.

9. Be consistent in reflecting a professional image in all your contacts, whether physical or virtual.

10. Differentiate yourself by including a personal touch in all your interactions. This is the mark of a true professional.

FACING ROADBLOCKS
TO SUCCESS

"If you run into a wall, don't turn around and give up. Figure out how to climb it, go through it, or work around it."

Michael Jordan

10

At the time of writing this final chapter, my family was celebrating my mum's 80th birthday. In between writing this book, I had been helping my siblings prepare for the big day. I planned a makeover for my mum, and my sister and I took her shopping and made a video with the help of my brother. As we were reviewing the video, flashes of our childhood memories brought joy and tears to my eyes. My mum is one woman who has faced huge roadblocks in her life. At the tender age of 17, she was matchmade to a 33-year-old entrepreneur (my dad) from China. He was widowed with an 8-year-old daughter in Singapore and another still in Hainan, China. They were a handsome pair, and except for the age gap, seemed like a perfect match. At 17, however, with little education and no time to enjoy teenage life, she was thrust into adulthood against her wishes.

Yet, diligently, she plunged into her role as wife and mother, and by the age of 32, she had seven children. I am the fourth child. When I was 32, I only had one child and was just starting to build my career. I cannot fathom how at 32, with eight children (including my eldest step-sister) to take care of, and with my father hardly being home, my mother could have survived it all. My father was a like a nomad (I suppose it's in the migrant blood), and at times, he would be overseas for months, and my mother would have to find her own way to make ends meet. During the day, she would take on jobs she could do from home, like laundry (in those days, it was done by hand), sewing (using her manual sewing machine), and even hairdressing. At night, when the older children were home to look after us toddlers, she would work as a waitress at a bar as the tips were good. You can say that it was quite a miracle, and through God's great blessing, that with only those bare hands, and no education or skills, she is where she is today. At 80, she has outlived my dad and my eldest sister, and is surrounded by her seven wonderful children and their spouses, 19 beautiful grandchildren and their spouses, and four great-grandchildren.

I am sure you've heard countless stories like that, and each one is special. If nothing else, I hope it drives home my main message in this final chapter:

no obstacles in life are so big that they can prevent you from achieving your dreams. If I've made sense to you as you've read through the chapters of this book, and if you have taken the steps to renew your professional image, you may have already begun to encounter some obstacles. Don't give up. This chapter will address some of the main roadblocks people face, and how we can overcome them.

Fast Fact

No obstacles are too big for us to overcome. They are there to challenge us to find creative solutions. We only become stronger and more resilient when we learn to face them squarely.

10 roadblocks to overcome

Let's return to the vehicle you drew in Chapter 2. This vehicle represents your professional image that will help drive you to your destination. I asked four questions about your vehicle:

What does it look like?

What does it sound like?

How does it behave?

Who are the passengers?

Now, as you review your roadmap again, and with your answers to these four questions, let's examine the potential obstacles that could block your journey to success:

1. ## What does your vehicle look like?

    If your answers to this question suggest a need to update your appearance, what is stopping you from doing so? You have completed the exercise on your brand values and know you need to project an image of your future. You know what changes are needed in your wardrobe. You may need further help in selecting the right colours and styles to create a new image. If you have not done so, are you facing some obstacles like many of my potential clients who have procrastinated on an image makeover? Here are some common ones I've come across:

    Roadblock #1: It costs too much

    "I can't afford an image consultant." "I'm unemployed." "Wait till I find a job, then I'll get an image makeover."

    Roadblock #2: I don't have time

    "I just can't find the time to go shopping." "I'm rushing out to work in the morning, and have no time to groom myself." "I work long hours, and have no time to even think about what to wear".

    Roadblock #3: It's not possible

    "I'm so set in my way of dressing, it's hard to change." "I'm already so old. It's too late to change." "I'm born like this. It's impossible to find beautiful clothes to fit me."

2. ## What does your vehicle sound like?

    If your sound is not consistent with your look, and your communication is not polished, you know it's going to be a long, slow journey to your destination. If your review of how you sound suggests you need to beef it up, and you have not taken any steps to do so, why are you waiting? Here are some more roadblocks I've often come across:

<u>Roadblock #4: I've failed too many times</u>

"I keep making mistakes in my speech, and just cannot seem to improve." "People always fall asleep during my presentations. It's just my style." "People laugh and make fun of me whenever I fumble."

<u>Roadblock #5: I get very nervous</u>

"I break out in a sweat when I have to speak in front of a crowd." "My knees shake and my hands tremble every time I make a presentation." "I cannot get over my nervousness."

<u>Roadblock #6: I have a language barrier</u>

"I am not fluent in English." "People just don't understand my accent." "It's hard to learn a new language at my age."

3.   **How does your vehicle behave?**

If you thought that changing your look or sound was difficult, it must be even more challenging when it comes to your behaviour. We agreed that we cannot change our personality, but we can change our behaviour if we want to. In your review of the behaviours that do not reflect your professional image, what challenges are you facing in "turning over a new leaf"? Here are some of the most challenging ones I've heard.

<u>Roadblock #7: It's still working for me</u>

"I still have my job. I'm content with the way I am." "People still accept me. I don't see why I should change." "People are used to the way I behave. It's fine."

<u>Roadblock #8: I'm too tired</u>

"Old habits die hard, and it's tiresome to correct them after so many years." "I have no energy to start learning new behaviours." "It's too stressful trying to remember the do's and don'ts."

4.   Who are the passengers?

In your review of the passengers who are travelling with you on this journey, have you considered how to enrol them to ensure a smooth ride? Just like a driver who is lost needs the help of a navigator to guide and support him, you too need passengers who can help you reach your destination with ease. Do your passengers pose any obstacles on your journey to success? Here are some potential obstacles:

<u>Roadblock #9: No one supports me</u>

"My family is so used to the old me, they think I'm insane to spend money on a makeover." "My colleagues think I'm trying to outdo them when I'm dressed up." "My boss refuses to sponsor my training."

<u>Roadblock #10: People keep criticising me</u>

"I'm never good enough. Every time I try to change, I'm still wrong." "Whenever there's a mistake, they blame me for it."

You may have more, but I believe these 10 cover most roadblocks I have come across. If you face all 10, don't worry too much. All of us face similar situations, and would have uttered at least one of these statements

at different times in moments of frustration or desperation. The important thing to note is that we have a choice: to do something about our situation or to allow ourselves to be overcome by it. If you choose to moan and groan, don't read further. You can read on if you decide to take control of your life and not let anything or anyone get in your way.

Aha! Moment

In facing any roadblock, I have a choice. I can choose to feel trapped and helpless, and not do anything, or I can choose to take control of the situation and look for a solution to remove it.

Removing roadblock #1: It costs too much

This is an age-old reason (or shall we say, excuse!) whenever someone refuses to buy something. It's the most useless response to a sales person: as they do not know if you want to buy, but cannot afford it, or you want to buy only if it's cheaper, or you're really not interested in buying. If your reason is not the latter, then we can address this roadblock here.

Let's assume you are interested and do indeed want to consult an image consultant for a makeover. Now if cost is an issue, have you sized up what the total cost is? If not, you do not know yet if you can afford it, or what alternative options there are to help you with financing. To address this concern of cost, here are some tips you can use:

1. **Decide what needs changing most.** Make a list of all the changes you need, e.g. a colour and style analysis, a new haircut, new suit, shoes etc. Divide into two categories, 'must have' and 'nice to have'. Within each list, prioritise according to what needs immediate change, e.g. if you are attending a job interview you might need a new suit, and that would be top priority.

2. **Estimate the cost.** Find out the cost of each item by calling up some suppliers to get a quote. When contacting an image consultant, be specific in stating your objectives and what you want to get out of a session. It is good to share your 'must have' and 'nice to have' list, so you can total up the two costs separately.

3. **Select the items you can afford.** Without blowing a hole in your pocket, select the 'must have' items you can afford according to your priorities. For the remaining items, indicate a timeframe you need to achieve a complete change.

4. **Review your current expenses.** If you cannot afford any of the 'must have' items, review your current expenses, and consider giving up some items temporarily. You will be surprised that you might actually

'create' some extra money from an unnecessary indulgence, which can be used for your 'must have' image makeover.

5. **Review other options.** If you still cannot find the extra money you need, consider other options of saving, making, or bartering, to build your funds for this important change. Be creative, and think of how you can contribute your talents or skills in exchange for some money or service.

Try This

Here's a cool way to create some instant 'wealth' without working, borrowing or stealing. After taking out your necessary expenses like rental, utilities, meals, or repayment of loans, make a list of other expenses you have incurred in the past year.

Example:

Eating out with friends:	$1,200
Clothes and accessories:	$3,000
Spa services:	$1,200
Facials:	$1,000
Hairstyling:	$1,200
Gym membership:	$2,400
Total:	**$10,000**

Now, review the expenses, and decide which items you can forego, reduce, or find alternatives for. Supposing you can reduce by half the expenses on eating out with friends and the gym membership (by entertaining and exercising at home), you would have instantly created $1,800!

Removing roadblock #2: I don't have time

If you have followed the steps to eradicate roadblock #1, you will more or less get a hang of how to address this one. We all know this to be true: everyone is busy, and no one has the time to do anything if it is not important to them. No matter how busy you are, you know some things just have to get done. So, this brings us back to whether making a change in your professional image matters to you now.

If it does, then there's no better time than now. Granted you have important work things to do, and you can't neglect the family. So, if getting a new image also matters to you, you have to similarly 'create' the time, just like you did with your money. List down all the things you must do and how much 'extra' time is required, e.g.

- Colour and style analysis (3 hours)

- Shopping (2 hours)

- Haircut (1 hour)

- Clear wardrobe (half a day)

- Brush up interview skills (half a day)

Now, block the time in your organiser for the next few weeks or months, and treat them like confirmed appointments that cannot be changed. If something else is more important than this, move it to another date but don't delete it. Even if you keep on moving it, at least it is there to remind you that an important matter still needs attention.

Removing roadblock #3: It's not possible

This is a killer one, and exists only in your head. It's the silent killer, because the voice that says "It's not possible" is coming from inside your head. I call him 'Brian', which is opposite for 'Brain'. You see, Brian really has no brain. And when you listen to Brian, you too have no brain. Listen to your brain, and recall all the heroic stories you know where miracles have happened. If you look at them closely, these miracles were only possible because someone believed. It's all in your belief system.

I have one simple solution for this problem: instead of saying, "It can't be done," ask the following questions:

What can be done?

How can I make it happen?

Who can help me make it happen?

When can it be done?

Removing roadblock #4: I've failed too many times

Who hasn't? Every success may have several failures. We experience it all the time. When you learn to ride a bicycle, you have to fall a few times before you realise why you fell, and learn how to balance yourself. If you gave up just after the last fall, you would never ride a bicycle again. Now, do you remember when was the last time you failed in something? Learn from the fall to find out what went wrong, and make that your last fall. Ask yourself these questions:

1. **What happened?** Describe the facts, not the emotion or the criticism. For example:

    At the last sales presentation, I forgot my first lines.

2. **What led to the situation?** Be specific about the action that could have caused it. For example:

   I did not write down my script. I did not rehearse the presentation.

3. **What could I have done differently?** Review the causes in point 2, and think of ways you can prevent the problem. For example:

   I must write down my introduction every time, and rehearse the night before, until I can do it without the script. I will keep my script with me as a back-up in case I blank out again.

Removing roadblock #5: I get very nervous

Nervousness is a symptom, not the roadblock itself. It is usually a sign of some underlying fear. If you are nervous before you go to a job interview, you may fear you can't answer a question. If you are nervous before a speech, you fear the audience may laugh at you. To remove this roadblock, address the fear instead of the nervousness. Here are some possible fears you might have and how to address them:

1. **Fear of the audience.** Find out about the audience, and arrive early to get to know them and put your fears at ease.

2. **Fear of difficult questions.** Anticipate what the difficult questions might be. Put yourself in the shoes of the recruiter, and prepare yourself with answers you know will address those questions.

3. **Fear of failure.** Identify what is needed to ensure success, and put your heart and soul into getting those areas right. Focus on winning, not losing.

4. **Fear you are not good enough.** Identify the standards of what is good enough. Devise a plan to reach those standards, and demonstrate how you have achieved them.

5. **Fear of the unknown.** This is a tough one! Find out what you don't know.

 Myth Buster

Nervousness is a physical problem and it can't be cured.

No matter how prepared I am, I still get nervous when I have to speak in front of a group. It is natural to be nervous, as it is the body's way of telling us there is a formidable obstacle ahead. It is a symptom of some fear in us. Address the specific fear, and overcome it by being prepared at all times in situations where you tend to get nervous.

Removing roadblock #6: I have a language barrier

Stop whining, and go take some language lessons! You are never too old to learn anything. You have a choice: either you learn to speak till you are understood, or you will be stuck in a 'communication jam' for a long time to come.

Removing roadblock #7: It's still working for me

This is my favourite: if it's still working for you, then stay where you are. Remember the roadmap where you indicated where you are, and where you are going. There is nowhere to go in your future if everything is working fine for you. If you are contented with what you are wearing now, the way you speak, and the way you behave, that's fine. The big question is: is it working for your future?

Danger Zone

Beware of being too comfortable when things are going well for you. Don't assume you will get that promotion just because you've worked very hard. Your image may be working for you now, but it may not take you to the next level.

Removing roadblock #8: I'm too tired

Stress is really not good for the soul, so if you feel stressed, you are facing a huge roadblock. There could be many causes of your stress, and we won't go there right now. If it is serious enough and other things in your life need attention, then seek professional help to get it sorted out. However, if you've always wanted a dramatic change in your professional image, take this as positive stress. Visualise yourself in your new image, looking, sounding and behaving like a professional. See the smile on your face, and on the faces of people around you. Feel the positive energy, and go for it!

Removing roadblock #9: No one supports me

This roadblock matters only if the people matter to you. Remember they are the passengers on board your vehicle, and you need each other to help you make it through the journey? If they don't matter, you don't need their support. So if you need training on a sales presentation, and your boss refuses to pay for it, find your own means to get it. Most likely, after you become a master salesman through no help of his, you can leave him to join the competition.

If the people matter dearly to you, then it's time for a one-to-one conversation to gain their support. Share with them your vision and goals, and what you need from them at each milestone. Excite them with your plans on how you can make it happen with their support.

Take the right passengers with you on your journey to success.

Removing roadblock #10: People keep criticising me

You can view criticism in two ways: one as constructive feedback, and the other as useless comments. Most people react to useless comments with more negative energy, mainly because they are not helpful and usually sound offensive. Don't waste your time and energy on useless criticism. Look for criticism that is constructive and phrased in a way that provides positive action. Use the feedback to review how you can make changes and create a positive impact on others.

Take the fast lane

On the highways in Singapore, there are huge electronic signboards that forewarn motorists of potential traffic obstacles ahead. This helps motorists to avoid the lanes in which an accident has occurred or a tree has fallen. The warnings are there to prevent a massive traffic jam, and to give ample notice so that motorists can make a detour. However, the strange phenomenon is that most motorists ignore these signs, and just get themselves deeper into the jam. So, what's the use of these signs if no one pays attention to them or does anything about them?

The same applies to you where your professional image is concerned. I believe we have established the potential impact that your image has on your future success. I also believe that we have set out clear guidelines for you to develop your roadmap, and how to take the fast lane to reach your destination. The signs are there. It is now up to you to get into the driver's seat, and take control. If you encounter any roadblocks, you know what to do. If you get lost and don't seem to be reaching your destination, review your roadmap to see where you need to make adjustments. One last note: remember to keep your vehicle looking, sounding and behaving professionally so that you reach your future destination.

Star Tips for removing roadblocks to success

1. Create 'extra wealth' by looking for unnecessary expenses you can forego.

2. Mark the dates for an important action you wish to take, and treat it like an appointment you cannot miss.

3. Believe that you can make things happen if you want to.

4. Learn from your past failures to find out how you can do things differently.

5. Identify what fear causes nervousness and address your specific fears.

6. Take action to improve your communication if it is a roadblock to success.

7. Determine if what is working for you now will also work for your future.

8. Visualise your future image to inject energy and overcome stress.

9. Enrol the important people in your life to share your roadmap to success.

10. Use constructive criticism to make changes and create a positive impact on others.

INDEX

ABOUT THE AUTHOR

Pang Li Kin AICI CIP is internationally recognised as a Certified Image Professional (CIP) by the Association of Image Consultants International (AICI). As one of the leading professionals in Singapore, Li Kin is a driving force behind the development of the image industry in the region. She serves as Vice President/President Elect on the 2009–2011 AICI South Asia-Singapore Chapter Board. Li Kin is also an appointed Success Coach with AICI globally, and is committed to helping aspiring image consultants grow their businesses across the world.

In recognition of her achievements in the industry, Li Kin received the coveted AICI Rising Star Award in 2008 and the Chapter Member of the Year Award in 2009. She started her Singapore company Potenxia Unlimited in 2002, helping individuals and companies develop their potential through their appearance, communication and interpersonal skills. Prior to that, Li Kin has had about 20 years of experience in business development, client servicing, leadership, as well as training and development. Her global experience spans 20 countries worldwide, having worked and trained with multi-national corporations across various industries including banking and finance, IT, manufacturing, telecommunications, petrochemical, retail, consumer goods, and the public sector.

Li Kin is a passionate speaker, trainer and facilitator who enjoys people, and customises each programme to her client's needs. She is trained by Image Master Lynne Marks, AICI CIM (London Image Institute, USA), and in the Colour Me a Season© System. She is also a qualified administrator of the Myers-Briggs Type Indicator (MBTI®) and holds a Bachelor of Social Sciences (Hons) degree (University of Singapore) and a Masters of Social Planning & Development (University of Queensland).

 **ST Training Solutions**

Success Skills Series

ST Training Solutions, based in Singapore, offers a wide range of popular, practical training programmes conducted by experienced, professional trainers. As CEO, Shirley Taylor takes a personal interest in working closely with trainers to ensure that each workshop is full of valuable tools, helpful guidelines and powerful action steps that will ensure a true learning experience for all participants. Some of the workshops offered are:

Powerful Business Writing Skills
Energise your E-mail Writing Skills
Success Skills for Secretaries and Support Staff
Successful Business Communication Skills
Creativity at Work
Speaking without Fear
Better Business English
Powerful People Skills
Activate your Listening Skills
Emotional Intelligence at Work
Win-Win Negotiation Skills
Business Etiquette Essentials
Dealing with Difficult People and Situations
Achieving Peak Performance by Improving your Memory
Enhance your Productivity with Speed-reading
Personal Effectiveness at Work
Professional Image: Your Roadmap to Success

Shirley Taylor is also host of a very popular annual conference called ASSAP — the Asian Summit for Secretaries and Admin Professionals — organised in April each year by ST Training Solutions.

Find out more about ST Training Solutions at www.shirleytaylortraining.com. Visit www.STSuccessSkills.com for additional resources.